Caitlin
Love you.
Keep movins!
Marjie

F O C U S

FOCUS

ELIMINATING DISTRACTIONS FOR
ENHANCED SPIRITUAL VISION

MARGIE FLEURANT

DESTINY IMAGE® PUBLISHERS, INC.

P.O. Box 310, Shippensburg, PA 17257-0310

"Promoting Inspired Lives."

This book and all other Destiny Image and Destiny Image Fiction books are available at Christian bookstores and distributors worldwide.

Cover design by Eileen Rockwell

For more information on foreign distributors, call 717-532-3040.

Reach us on the Internet: www.destinyimage.com.

ISBN 13 TP: 978-0-7684-0897-3

ISBN 13 eBook: 978-0-7684-0898-0

For Worldwide Distribution, Printed in the U.S.A.

1 2 3 4 5 6 7 8 / 20 19 18 17 16

DEDICATION

I dedicate this book to the apostolic leaders, prophets, and teachers in my life. Thank you for pouring into me and my ministry through your teaching, training, mentoring, and prophetic words. You have passed the baton on to me, and it is my hope to pass the baton on to the next generation of leaders.

CONTENTS

INTRODUCTION

Few have vision. Live by what you see with
the eyes of your spirit. The eyes of your spirit
are the windows into the spirit realm.
—RICK JOYNER

When Saul encountered Jesus on the road to Damascus, his life changed in a moment. Reality as he had known it suddenly died, and he discovered a new reality in Christ. The brilliant vision of Jesus—in which He revealed the truth of who He really is to Saul—temporarily made Saul physically blind but opened his spiritual eyes. In a very real sense, he became blind so that he could truly see. Several days later, when Ananias prayed for Saul and his vision was restored, something like scales fell from Saul's eyes. These were a manifestation of not only physical blindness but also spiritual blindness. Both left Saul that day, and he began his journey toward his destiny as one of the greatest apostles of the gospel.

Like Saul, when our eyes are spiritually opened, we receive the vision needed to have clear focus. This focus puts us on the path to fulfilling our destiny. Of course, staying focused is not easy. If it was, everyone would do it. The truth is, we are bombarded with distractions from the enemy designed to make us spiritually blind. These distractions pull our eyes away from the vision of Jesus and fill our minds and hearts with lesser things. If we do not deal with them, they have the potential to sideline us and prevent us from accomplishing God's plans for our lives. For this reason, it is crucial for us to self-examine, to consider what we are looking at and whether we are living focused lives. As Paul wrote to the believers at Corinth:

> *Examine yourselves to see whether you are in the faith; test yourselves. Do you not realize that Christ Jesus is in you—unless, of course, you fail the test?* (2 Corinthians 3:15)

The nature of deception is that we are deceived. We cannot see the deception—unless we invite God's correction in our lives. He knows what has the potential to keep us from our destinies, and He warns us about those distractions. Only He can open our eyes to deception lurking in our corners. The question is, will we listen? Will we pay attention and willingly submit to His correction? If we will, He will show us *what we are really looking at,* and He will help us refocus on His vision.

Then, like Jesus, we will be empowered to run our race with endurance:

> *Therefore, since we are surrounded by such a great cloud of witnesses, let us throw off everything that hinders and the sin that so easily entangles. And let us run with perseverance the race marked out for us, fixing our eyes on Jesus, the pioneer and perfecter of faith. For the joy set before him he endured the cross,*

scorning its shame, and sat down at the right hand of the throne of God (Hebrews 12:1-2).

This is how we overcome the distractions of life—by examining ourselves and refocusing on God's spiritual vision. The need to self-examine is never finished. In different seasons of life, we will encounter different distractions. The breakthroughs we need are uncovered in the secret place with our loving Father, who knows and desires the very best for us.

In Part 1 of this book, we will consider how to restore our spiritual focus so we can live successfully according to Heaven's standards. In Part 2, we will look at ten of the most common distractions that keep Christians from focusing on God's spiritual vision for their lives. Self-examination is not easy, but it is always worth the pain. Join me on this quest for truth at any cost and the joy of running with perseverance the race marked out before us!

Part 1

---•---

Restoring
Spiritual Focus

———————•———————

Chapter 1

BETWEEN HEAVEN AND EARTH

*My home is in heaven. I'm just
travelling through this world.*
—BILLY GRAHAM

The enemy uses many tools against us to try to distract us from God's vision for our lives. (We will look at ten of these distractions in Part 2 of this book.) Many of us, without realizing it, have at various times been disillusioned by these lies from our enemy. We've given in to offense, people-pleasing, self-absorption, focus on the past, the easy road, the noise of the enemy, discouragement, the treasures of the world, reliance on our own works, or weariness. In so doing, we've lost our focus and turned our eyes from God's purpose for our lives. Thankfully, even when this happens, we can still overcome the enemy's distractions and regain our vision.

A big part of shaking free of these lies is found in the realization of our identity as those who live between two worlds. As humans in physical bodies, we live in the physical realm of earth. But, the Bible tells us we are also spiritual beings who are seated in heavenly places with Jesus (see Eph. 2:6). When we are born again, Heaven becomes our true home, yet we continue to live on earth. This position between two worlds can be incredibly powerful—if we understand its purpose and are able to see above the temporal circumstances of life on earth. However, for many of us, this goes against our natural inclinations. We have difficulty looking upward, because we are focused on what is happening all around.

While it may be difficult to look at life this way, it is absolutely vital. Right now, as believers on earth, we live as light in the midst of darkness. We live as God's spiritual army on earth, here to expand His Kingdom and eventually overcome the darkness with His light and life. This is what the prophet Isaiah prophesied:

> *Arise [from the depression and prostration in which circumstances have kept you—rise to a new life]! Shine (be radiant with the glory of the Lord), for your light has come, and the glory of the Lord has risen upon you! For behold, darkness shall cover the earth, and dense darkness [all] peoples, but the Lord shall arise upon you [O Jerusalem], and His glory shall be seen on you* (Isaiah 60:1-2 AMP).

God's glory is rising upon the Church, and more and more, believers are stepping into their true identity as sons and daughters of God. The Kingdom of God is expanding in the earth; approximately one-third of the people alive on earth today are believers. Simultaneously, the darkness in the world is increasing as Satan desperately attempts to overthrow

God's ever-expanding Kingdom. This is the reality we live in—the dual nature of the two worlds we reside in. This should not cause us to fear or despair. Instead, we must follow Jesus' advice for hard times: *"Stand up and lift up your heads, because your redemption is drawing near"* (Luke 21:28). To do this, we must first understand our identity and calling while we live on earth.

EARTH: THIS PRESENT WORLD

One thing that sets Christians apart from others is the belief that we are citizens of another world and this present world is not our true home. As Jesus said, *"My kingdom is not of this world"* (John 18:36). It follows, then, that we will not necessarily feel at home in this world. The apostle John told early believers, *"Do not be surprised, my brothers and sisters, if the world hates you"* (1 John 3:13). It is natural for people to dislike or be suspicious of outsiders. In a very real sense, we are outsiders in this world, because our focus and priorities are different. Our culture is not rooted in earth but in Jesus, who tells us what it looks like to live in His Kingdom. Thus, when we face persecution, whether physical or social, we can find strength in our identity as sons and daughters of a God who promises to reward us for faithfully living for Him on earth. As Jesus told His followers: *"Rejoice and be glad, because great is your reward in heaven, for in the same way they persecuted the prophets who were before you"* (Matt. 5:12).

Jesus was the first one to experience life as a human on earth, yet as a citizen of Heaven. About this, He said, *"You are from below; I am from above. You are of this world; I am not of this world"* (John 8:23). As His followers, born again by His Spirit, we are also now *"from above."* Now, like Him, we live as foreigners in this world. We can never fully belong, because our identity and purpose are rooted in a Kingdom that is not of this world. While the people of this world chase after wealth and pleasure and other temporal pursuits that have won their hearts, our perspective is informed by these words from Jesus: *"What good will it be for someone to gain the whole world, yet forfeit their soul? Or what can anyone give in exchange for their soul?"* (Matt. 16:26). The things of this world are no longer our highest priority, because we have raised our eyes to look beyond the temporal into the eternal.

As a result, we are able to live bravely and maintain focus, no matter what life throws our way. The apostle Paul described it this way:

> *Therefore we do not lose heart. Though outwardly we are wasting away, yet inwardly we are being renewed day by day. For our light and momentary troubles are achieving for us an eternal glory that far outweighs them all. So we fix our eyes not on what is seen, but on what is unseen, since what is seen is temporary, but what is unseen is eternal* (2 Corinthians 4:16-18).

In other words, we interpret the temporal experiences of life through the lenses of eternity. This enables us to rise above painful circumstances, to hold loosely to our worldly possessions, and to rise above the worldly passions that drive the people of this world. This is exactly what John meant when he wrote:

> *Do not love the world or anything in the world. If anyone loves the world, love for the Father is not in them. For everything in the world—the lust of the flesh, the lust of the eyes, and the pride of life—comes not from the Father but from the world* (1 John 2:15-16).

Similarly, Jesus talked about how the cares of this world can cause us to be ineffective in our calling to advance His Kingdom on earth. He said, *"The worries of this life, the deceitfulness of wealth and the desires for other things come in and choke the word, making it unfruitful"* (Mark 4:19). This doesn't mean we should become hermits who do not enjoy any earthly pleasures or comforts. God has given us many things for our enjoyment (see 1 Tim. 6:17). What it does mean is that the comforts and pleasures of this life should never become more important to us than our calling in the Kingdom of God. Perspective makes all the difference.

The apostle Paul said it this way: *"Whoever sows to please their flesh, from the flesh will reap destruction; whoever sows to please the Spirit, from the Spirit will reap eternal life"* (Gal. 6:8). In other words, the priorities of our hearts determine the fruit we will reap. As believers, our priority should always be to obey God and fulfill His purpose for our lives.

The life of Paul gives us a tremendous example of how to live with an eternal perspective. After he encountered Jesus and said yes to his calling, Paul lived his life to fulfill that calling, while also anticipating his departure from earth to Heaven. While he still needed (and even enjoyed) the physical elements of life—like food and rest, provision for his body, and close friendships—he was not entangled in the affairs of this present world. He experienced both abundance and lack, and neither could shake him from his eternal focus (see Phil. 4:12). His eyes were always fixed on the ultimate prize of his life in Christ. Thus, he could say to his spiritual son, Timothy:

> *Join with me in suffering, like a good soldier of Christ Jesus. No one serving as a soldier gets entangled in civilian affairs, but rather tries to please his commanding officer* (2 Timothy 2:3-4).

He lived with the mindset of a soldier, always focused on the big-picture purpose and the end goal for his life. Part of what makes soldiers effective members of an army is their ability to put their personal interests and lives aside and give their all, evenunto the death, for the cause of their nation. In the same way, we as believers get to live with a higher purpose than our own individual lives. We get to live for the goals of the Kingdom of God and freely give ourselves in pursuit of those goals. When we do, we will approach the end of life like Paul did:

> *For I am already being poured out like a drink offering, and the time for my departure is near. I have fought the good fight, I have finished the race, I have kept the faith. Now there is in store for me the crown of righteousness, which the Lord, the righteous Judge, will award to me on that day—and not only to me, but also to all who have longed for his appearing* (2 Timothy 4:6-8).

Truly, at the center of Paul's lifestyle was a focus on the Kingdom of God and his eternal purpose as a soldier called to advance that Kingdom on earth. We are called to do the same, but to make that counter-cultural choice, we must first be convinced of the importance of the Kingdom of God and our mission within it.

ETERNITY: THE KINGDOM OF GOD

The reality is, when we accepted Jesus in our hearts and asked Him to be both Lord and Savior of our lives, we stepped from one world into another. In a moment, we became citizens of Heaven: *"But our citizenship is in heaven. And we eagerly await a Savior from there, the Lord Jesus Christ"* (Phil. 3:20). We transitioned from being enemies of the Kingdom of God— those Paul described in this way: *"Their destiny is destruction, their god is their stomach, and their glory is in their shame. Their mind is set on earthly things"* (Phil. 3:19)—to being ambassadors of that Kingdom on earth. In Jesus, we received eternal life here and now, even while we live in our physical bodies. Jesus came to give us *zoe* life (eternal life)[1] to the full (see John 10:10). This identity as ambassadors of God's Kingdom, filled with eternal life, gives us a purpose that should inform everything we do.

This means a change in our priorities, where the values of Heaven become more important to us than the values of earth. As Paul said, *"Set your minds on things above, not on earthly things"* (Col. 3:2). This is important because, as Paul also said, the things of this earth cannot inherit an eternal Kingdom: *"I declare to you, brothers and sisters, that flesh and blood cannot inherit the kingdom of God, nor does the perishable inherit the imperishable"* (1 Cor. 15:50). All our earthly achievements apart from Christ hold no eternal value, because they are temporal. They belong to this world and are incapable of transcending into eternity. By contrast, our achievement for the Kingdom—our obedience to God's call for our lives, whatever that looks like for each of us individually—carries eternal significance. Thus, our focus must not be on this world but on the things of eternity and on doing the will of God.

Paul wrote about this reality in his first letter to the Corinthians, telling them about the importance of building well upon the foundation of Jesus Christ and His Kingdom during our lives on earth:

> *By the grace God has given me, I laid a foundation as a wise builder, and someone else is building on it. But each one should build with care. For no one can lay any foundation other than the one already laid, which is Jesus Christ. If anyone builds on this*

foundation using gold, silver, costly stones, wood, hay or straw, their work will be shown for what it is, because the Day will bring it to light. It will be revealed with fire, and the fire will test the quality of each person's work. If what has been built survives, the builder will receive a reward. If it is burned up, the builder will suffer loss but yet will be saved— even though only as one escaping through the flames (1 Corinthians 3:10-15).

Eternity will reveal the quality of the work we do for the Kingdom on earth. This work does not determine our salvation (which is by faith alone), but it does determine the reward we will receive in Heaven. During the span of our lives on earth, we have the opportunity to build the Kingdom in partnership with God in a way that we cannot after we go to Heaven. So many people waste the short years of their lives chasing after the comforts and pleasures of this life instead of using their time on earth to gain eternal treasure. When our eyes are fixed on eternity, we will be driven by God's desire for our lives, not the desires of this temporal earth.

The more this is true in our lives, the more we will walk in great grace, just like the early Church did (see Acts 4:33; 17:6). Though they faced severe persecution and many other hurdles to their faith, they maintained their focus on the eternal Kingdom of God and, as a result, were able to persevere and overcome. As bold and strong men and women of God—who were driven by purpose, vision, and prayer—they lived their lives for eternity. They lived out of the reality that *"the kingdom of God is not a matter of eating and drinking, but of righteousness, peace and joy in the Holy Spirit"* (Rom. 14:17). As a result of being rooted in the righteousness, peace, and joy of God, no matter the circumstances around them they were able to also live in the reality that *"the kingdom of God is not a matter of talk but of power"* (1 Cor. 4:20).

Such eternity-focused living is dependent on two revelations about our identity: first, that Heaven is our real home, and second, that God is our real Father.

1. Heaven Our Home

As humans, we find a great deal of significance and identity from our place of origin—our families, our nations, even our neighborhoods. To a degree, we are a product of where we come from, so it makes sense that we would derive self-worth—manifested in either pride or shame—from our origins. We see this reality throughout human history. Many people have found their purpose and drive in life from their origin; it is our default. Thus, those who come from privileged families, nations, and neighborhoods tend to view themselves as influencers who are worthy of respect and capable of accomplishing their dreams. By contrast, those who grow up disadvantaged often have great mental and emotional hurdles to overcome, because they come from a place that teaches them to look down on themselves and to doubt their ability to succeed.

For believers, regardless of our origin in the natural, when we are born again through faith in Jesus, we are restored to our real origin as members of God's family. Our origin is no longer based on earthly realities but on the eternal reality of our citizenship in Heaven. Now, home is not a place on a physical map of earth; it is a place in God's heavenly abode. Jesus promised us, *"My Father's house has many rooms; if that were not so, would I have told you that I am going there to prepare a place for you?"* (John 14:2).

Imagine this scenario. A neglected, abused, and unloved child from the slums is adopted by a wealthy family. When that child first arrives at her new home, she discovers a beautiful room arranged and decorated just for her. It is the new place where she belongs, and though it may take some time for her to shake her former slum-child identity, her new home will begin to create in her a new identity. She will begin to see herself as a valuable and loved child worthy of being protected and provided for. In the same way, we are translated from the kingdom of darkness into the Kingdom of light, and we find a new identity in our origin as citizens of Heaven. It is now the one place where we most belong. As a result, it should inform everything we do while on earth.

The truth is, our home in Heaven is more real than our home on earth. Our heavenly home is eternal, but our earthly home will pass away. Thus, for us to understand our identity based on our heavenly origin, Heaven and the spiritual realm must be more real to us than the physical realities we discern with our five senses. As eternal beings, the only thing that currently separates us from our home in Heaven is our physical bodies. This is not a bad thing, of course. God gave us our bodies and our physical existence for an eternal purpose, but we will only be able to live out that purpose when we are continually aware of our real home in Heaven and the identity it gives us.

2. God Our Father

Just as Heaven is our real home, God is also our real Father. We no longer need to find identity in the love and approval (or lack thereof) of our natural parents, because we have a Father in Heaven who loves us more than we can ever comprehend. And He believes in us enough to send His Son to die and redeem us back into relationship with Him. No matter what we have done, He calls us His children and invites us back into His family. This reality will change us. It will cause us to live with an eternal perspective rooted in a desire to please the Father who so dearly loves us.

When we are born into the spirit, we become children of the Father of spirits, as the writer of Hebrews said: *"Moreover, we have all had human fathers who disciplined us and we respected them for it. How much more should we submit to the Father of spirits and live"* (Heb. 12:9). Jesus was the first person to call God His Father, and as co-heirs with Him, we now call God our Father, too. When Jesus' parents lost track of Him for a few days and then found Him in the temple, Jesus said to them,

> *And He said to them, How is it that you had to look for Me? Did you not see and know that it is necessary [as a duty] for Me to be in My Father's house and [occupied] about My Father's business?* (Luke 2:49 AMP)

Like Jesus, we too should live to fulfill the will of our Father on earth. We too must be about our Father's business.

When we understand who we are from Heaven's perspective, this will be our natural response. The apostle John described it this way: *"This is how love is made complete among us so that we will have confidence on the day of judgment: In this world we are like Jesus"* (1 John 4:17). Love is made complete in us as we become like Jesus in this world. As our identity as children of God manifests, we begin to look and act very much like Jesus. He will be more real to us than the people around us, and the reality of who He is and who we are in Him will cause us to live for eternity.

LIVING FOR ETERNITY

When we live from our heavenly identity, we will understand God's value system; we will see that success on earth does not always look the same as success in Heaven. Often, the characteristics and values that will make us influencers on earth will be stumbling blocks to being influencers in Heaven. Simply put—what looks good on earth is not the same as what looks good in Heaven. The things that seem small and insignificant on earth may be the very things that qualify us for a crown in Heaven. The value system of Heaven is different, and as a result Heaven has different history books than the ones we read here on earth. Earthly histories pass away, but the books kept in Heaven will last forever. Because of this, we must ask ourselves, "What is Heaven recording about my life?"

The unfortunate reality, for many believers, is that *if we truly had our focus on eternity, we would be living our lives differently.* We need Heaven's perspective to inform our lives on earth. This is what the psalmist meant when he wrote, *"Teach us to number our days, that we may gain a heart of wisdom"* (Ps. 90:12). Remembering the shortness of our time on earth and the purpose for our existence here will help us to live for eternity. God could have orchestrated it that when we receive His offer of forgiveness and eternal life we immediately leave our earthly existence and enter Heaven. But He didn't. That means our lives on earth have a purpose. The question is, do we want to have a greater reputation on earth or in Heaven? The apostle Paul had a reputation in the spiritual realm, and as a result, his life on earth produced great eternal fruit. We see this so clearly in the story of the seven sons of Sceva:

> *Some Jews who went around driving out evil spirits*
> *tried to invoke the name of the Lord Jesus over those*
> *who were demon-possessed. They would say, "In the*

name of the Jesus whom Paul preaches, I command you to come out." Seven sons of Sceva, a Jewish chief priest, were doing this. One day the evil spirit answered them, "Jesus I know, and Paul I know about, but who are you?" Then the man who had the evil spirit jumped on them and overpowered them all. He gave them such a beating that they ran out of the house naked and bleeding (Acts 19:13-16).

God wants all of His children to have this sort of reputation in the spiritual realm. He wants us to take our focus from this world and to focus instead on eternity and the things that please Him. In so doing, we will be able to live our lives on this earth as effective ambassadors of God's Kingdom, and we will fulfill our destiny in Him.

Through the distractions we will discuss in the second half of this book, Satan tries to get us off course from God's calling for our lives. He tries to shift our focus to earth's priorities and value systems. But God wants us to be guided by eternity, so that when we see Him face to face He will be able to say to us, "Well done good and faithful servants," and we will be worthy of the eternal rewards He desires to give us (see Matt. 25:23). Then we will experience the eternal home that has been ours all along.

This is why we must not live for this temporal world. In light of this, my personal motto has become: "I don't live for this world; I live every day in the light of eternity." As I started living based on that reality, my heart began to change. I began to feel what Paul described in Philippians 1:22-24:

If I am to go on living in the body, this will mean fruitful labor for me. Yet what shall I choose? I do not know! I am torn between the two: I desire to depart and be with Christ, which is better by far;

27

but it is more necessary for you that I remain in the body.

I desired to depart to be with Christ (which is far better) while also recognizing that it was important for the Church and for my friends and family that I remain on earth a while longer. This realization caused me to adjust my thinking again, to remind myself that my time on earth is not complete yet. As a matter of fact, I have faith that I will live into my nineties! It *is* possible to become so spiritually minded that we become of no earthly good. It's all about the balance between the two worlds—finding our identity and purpose in Heaven, yet living our lives fully here on earth until God calls us home. It is natural, when we begin to realize that Heaven is our home and God is our Father, to want to go to be with Him in eternity. Yet He has important plans and purposes for us here on earth.

Not long ago, I heard God say to me, "I want to work a work in your day that, if I told it to you, it would seem like a dream." He has great things in store for us, not only in eternity but also here on earth, as we live with an eternal perspective. I believe the best years are ahead of the Church. He is training, preparing, and raising us up as those who know who we are as citizens of Heaven and, as a result, can powerfully advance His Kingdom on earth. This is exactly what Paul prayed for when he wrote:

> *May our Lord Jesus Christ himself and God our Father, who loved us and by his grace gave us eternal encouragement and good hope, encourage your hearts and strengthen you in every good deed and word* (2 Thessalonians 2:16-17).

The realities of eternity and our identity in Christ are designed to strengthen and encourage us so that we can fight the good fight on this earth. Truly, He has given us a good hope that can and should inform every day of our lives, no matter what is happening around us.

PRAYER OF REFLECTION

Lord, help me to daily be aware of my position between the two realms of Heaven and earth. Remind me that, though I physically live on earth and experience the realities of earth with my five senses, my real home and identity are in Heaven. I want my life to be guided by this revelation of eternity so that I will fulfill Your plans for me.

Chapter 2

---●---

LIVING FROM THE SPIRIT

We need a baptism of clear seeing.
We desperately need seers who
can see through the mist—Christian
leaders with prophetic vision.
—A.W. TOZER

Once we recognize our position as citizens of Heaven who live as ambassadors of the Kingdom on earth, we will be ready to learn to live from the spirit realm. This does not mean simply living with eternal perspective, as we talked about in Chapter 1, but also learning how to use our spiritual senses to understand and engage the spirit realm. So many of us are used to understanding reality primarily through our five physical senses, but the truth is, as born-again believers, the physical world is not our greatest reality. Instead, even while we live in the physical realm, our greatest reality is in the spiritual realm around us. Not only is Heaven our true home, but the spirit realm is our true reality. This realm, though often unseen to our natural eyes, can be discerned by our spiritual senses.

During His life on earth, Jesus was able to discern spiritual realities; He often spiritually knew the condition of people's hearts (see Mark 2:8). This wasn't because He was God in the flesh but because the Spirit of God lived in Him and His human spirit was fully in tune with God. We know this because the apostles also demonstrated this ability to see into spiritual realities. When Simon the Sorcerer asked Peter to give him the power to impart the Spirit through the laying on of hands, Peter rebuked him based on what he discerned to be in Simon's heart: *"For I see that you are full of bitterness and captive to sin"* (Acts 8:23).

Not surprisingly, one of the gifts of the Spirit listed in the Bible is the gift of discerning of spirits (see 1 Cor. 12:10). What this means is that God intends for us to be able to see into the spirit realm and discern what is going on with spiritual forces and in people's hearts. As ambassadors of Heaven, we need to be aware of what is happening around us, because:

> *Our struggle is not against flesh and blood, but against the rulers, against the authorities, against the powers of this dark world and against the spiritual forces of evil in the heavenly realms* (Ephesians 6:12).

Much more is happening around us than what we can see with our physical eyes, and God intends for us to be aware of it. He has made us to see into the spirit realm, both good and evil, and to live from that realm. When we do, we are able to more effectively impact the natural realm.

OUR SPIRIT IDENTITY

To understand this, we first need to realize that our primary identity is as spiritual beings. Paul said it this way: *"You, however, are not in the realm of the flesh but are in the realm of the Spirit, if indeed the Spirit of God lives in you"* (Rom. 8:9). Though the spirit is not the part of us we see with our eyes, it is the part of us that is more central and real to who we are. Jesus described our spiritual nature by comparing us to the wind: *"The wind blows wherever it pleases. You hear its sound, but you cannot tell where it comes from or where it is going. So it is with everyone born of the Spirit"* (John 3:8). Our spirits are unseen, but they are the driving force of our lives.

Simply put, we are spirit beings who have souls (minds, wills, and emotions) and who live in physical bodies. With our spirits we contact the spirit realm, with our souls we contact the intellectual realm, and with our bodies we contact the physical realm. The Bible tells us our triune beings (spirit, soul, and body) can be divided (see 1 Thess. 5:23; Heb. 4:12), yet the entirety of our beings is important. This is why Paul prayed for the whole person to be sanctified:

> *May God himself, the God of peace, sanctify you through and through. May your whole spirit, soul and body be kept blameless at the coming of our Lord Jesus Christ* (1 Thessalonians 5:23).

When we accept Jesus into our hearts, our spirits come alive as new creations (see 2 Cor. 5:17-21; John 3:3-8). Our spirits are the part of us that are born again and have an intimate connection to God, who is a Spirit. As Paul put it: *"But whoever is united with the Lord is one with him in spirit"* (1 Cor. 6:17). When we are born again, our spirits are knit together with God. After our spirits are born again, they take leadership of our beings and are designed to guide our souls and bodies into alignment with the Kingdom of God. In other words, God wants our souls to be renewed and restored by the Word of God, and our bodies should become living sacrifices to God (see Rom. 12:1-2; Ps. 23:2-3). This is the process needed to make us into people who live from the spirit realm and focus on the desires of the Spirit rather than the desires of our souls and bodies. As Paul wrote:

> *Those who live according to the flesh have their minds set on what the flesh desires; but those who live in accordance with the Spirit have their minds set on what the Spirit desires. The mind governed by the flesh is death, but the mind governed by the Spirit is life and peace* (Romans 8:5-6).

However, the fact that our spirits are reborn as new creations does not necessarily mean our souls and bodies follow suit. It is a decision we as individuals have to make. It is up to us whether we will submit our whole selves to the leadership of God's Spirit in connection with our spirits, or whether we will continue to live according to the desires of our souls and bodies. Sanctification is not an instant experience but a process of submitting our lives to God's leadership. Thus, some believers take the first step in receiving Jesus as their Savior, but they never truly allow Him to be Lord in their lives.

To believers like this, Paul wrote, *"Brothers and sisters, I could not address you as people who live by the Spirit but as people who are still worldly—mere infants in Christ"* (1 Cor. 3:1). These believers had not matured as God intends, and therefore, they were not living by the spirit but by the flesh. To the immature believers in Galatia, Paul also wrote:

> *So I say, walk by the Spirit, and you will not gratify the desires of the flesh. For the flesh desires what is*

contrary to the Spirit, and the Spirit what is contrary to the flesh. They are in conflict with each other, so that you are not to do whatever you want. But if you are led by the Spirit, you are not under the law (Galatians 5:16-18).

These believers were using their freedom in Christ to indulge the flesh when they should have been using it to live by the Spirit. Paul then went on to list the fruit of life in the Spirit—love, joy, peace, patience, kindness, goodness, faithfulness, and self-control. These evidences of the Spirit show us the importance of living from the spirit realm. God's character cannot be manifested in us unless we live by the Spirit, and our true identity and purpose cannot be derived from any part of us other than our spirits. The real "us" is found in our spirits, what the apostle Peter called *"your inner self"* (1 Pet. 3:4) or *"the hidden person of the heart"* (NKJV). Only when our souls and bodies are submitted to the leadership of our spirits will we be able to walk in our destiny.

In the words of the apostle Paul, *"Since we live by the Spirit, let us keep in step with the Spirit"* (Gal. 5:25), and *"So then, just as you received Christ Jesus as Lord, continue to live your lives in him"* (Col. 2:6). For each one of us, it is a choice. We must decide what realm we will live from and for. Only when we live from the spirit realm and are motivated by spiritual realities will we be able to walk in our destiny as children of God.

SPIRITUAL EYESIGHT

A crucial part of living in the spirit realm is seeing with our spiritual eyes. These spiritual eyes are the windows into the spirit realm, and as new creations, we are created to see with them. Our spiritual eyes are created to see like peregrine falcons, who have some of the best eyesight in all of creation.

These large birds of prey can see eight times more clearly than humans. This enables them to fly high in the air while looking for prey, to focus clearly on an object while in flight, and to accurately dive at 200 miles per hour in order to catch their prey.[2] Because of the sharpness of their vision, they are able to move with tremendous speed (they are the fastest members of the animal kingdom) without losing their clarity of perception. Falcons are truly impressive birds, and in them we can see a picture of the great insight God has put within our spiritual nature.

Our spiritual eyes are made to see with great depth of understanding and perception, so that we can respond accurately to the spiritual world around us and, when necessary, move with great confidence and speed in order to do the works of God's Kingdom. However, many Christians have never learned how to cultivate their spiritual eyesight, and as a result, they move through life guided primarily by their natural vision. This makes it much harder to genuinely live for eternity, because we live according to what we see.

The apostle Paul recognized the importance of spiritual vision, and he prayed that believers would have it:

> *I keep asking that the God of our Lord Jesus Christ, the glorious Father, may give you the Spirit of wisdom and revelation, so that you may know him better. I pray that the eyes of your heart may be enlightened in order that you may know the hope to which he has called you, the riches of his glorious inheritance in his holy people, and his incomparably great power for us who believe* (Ephesians 1:17-19).

The phrase *"eyes of your heart"* refers to our spiritual eyes. These are needed for spiritual wisdom and revelation.

Without our spiritual eyes, we cannot comprehend these three critical realities:

1.   The hope of our calling

2.   The riches of our inheritance

3.   God's power at work in our lives

Without spiritual vision, we will never recognize that our calling as ambassadors of God's Kingdom on this earth is actually better than any earthly pursuit. Without spiritual vision, we will never see how incredible God's rewards are; we will not value the spiritual inheritance He has reserved for us. And without spiritual vision, we will not truly believe that God's power in us is greater than any earthly power and any power of the enemy. The danger (and loss) involved in not seeing these three truths is enormous. An inability to see with our spiritual eyes will inhibit us from walking in our identity as children of God and our calling as ambassadors of His Kingdom. We see this in the example of the two disciples who encountered Jesus on the road to Emmaus but did not recognize Him. Not until He opened their eyes were they able to see who they were talking with. *"Then their eyes were opened and they recognized him, and he disappeared from their sight"* (Luke 24:31).

The eyes of our hearts are windows to the realm of the spirit. When our spiritual eyes are open, we will recognize spiritual truth. We will know our identity, our inheritance, and our power, and that power is a really big deal. In the verses following his prayer for the enlightenment of the eyes of our hearts, Paul highlighted the scope of the power God has placed in believers:

> *That power is the same as the mighty strength he exerted when he raised Christ from the dead and*

seated him at his right hand in the heavenly realms
(Ephesians 1:19-20).

When we recognize the power of God within us, we realize that, truly, with God *nothing* is impossible. Thus, we are able to look at life according to the potential of His power at work in us rather than the lesser powers of sickness or poverty or other difficulties. The question is, *what are we looking at?* What we look at will determine what we believe in. If we look with our spiritual eyes at Jesus and the things of His Kingdom, we will not be shaken by mere earthly realities. Instead, we will be filled *"with the knowledge of his will through all the wisdom and understanding that the Spirit gives"* (Col. 1:9). Then we will see in the spirit with the depth and clarity of the falcon.

The Old Testament prophet Jeremiah was one who saw prophetically with his spirit eyes. When God asked Jeremiah, "What do you see?" Jeremiah would see an image that spoke prophetically about the future (see Jer. 1:11-16). When he saw a budding almond tree, it wasn't just a budding almond tree. It was a promise that God was watching to see that His word was fulfilled. This shows us that what we see may look one way to our physical eyes but portray a different reality to our spiritual eyes.

For example, in early 1981, God gave me a vision for the East Coast of the United States as I was reading Ezekiel 36:33-38. In context, these verses speak of the assurance of Israel's restoration, but God used them to speak to me about my call and assignment on the East Coast. As I read those verses, my heart began to burn with the love of God for the East Coast, and the Scriptures seemed to light up or jump off the page of my Bible. I felt the witness of the Holy Spirit, and He imparted vision to me that has sustained me to this day. The Lord said to me:

No one wants to come to the East Coast. They all
say it's too hard, and the people are not responsive.
I want you to teach My people about prayer, and as
a result, the spiritual atmosphere will change, and
the ground of their hearts will be tilled. Intercession will till the ground of their hearts. I want to
do a new thing on the East Coast, to fortify the
area spiritually so I can send a revival. Where sin
abounds, My grace will so much more abound,
and the East Coast will become like the Garden of
Eden.

At that time, I did not know that New Jersey is called the
Garden State or that one of the main roads in New Jersey is
the Garden State Parkway. I have held on to this vision from
God for almost thirty-five years. Whenever I minister under
the anointing and operate as a seer, I see a major move of
God coming to the East Coast. I have faith that it will happen
because I have seen it with the eyes of my spirit. This is the
power of spiritual vision. I am able to see this in the spirit,
and absolutely believe in it, before it has manifested in the
physical realm.

Because of this, when I go to churches on the East Coast,
God uses me to breathe life into them and impart to them
this vision for their region, so they can keep praying without becoming weary (see Luke 18:1). When we are driven by
spiritual vision, even when what we see with the eyes of our
spirit tarries, we will continue to pray until the unseen realm
manifests in the visible realm. While I attended Rhema Bible
College, I often heard Kenneth E. Hagin talk about how the
spirit realm is more real than the natural realm. Because the
spirit realm was here first, he said, if we want to change something in the natural, we must go to the spirit. The true reality
is always what we perceive in our spirits. This is why, as new

creations in Christ, we must live according to what we see in the spirit—not what we see in the natural.

ENGAGING DESTINY

All of us face times in our lives when we question who we are and what we are here for. We struggle to find our calling and purpose in this life. Usually this happens because we have started looking at life according to our physical sight rather than our spiritual sight. We have stopped (or maybe never started) engaging the eyes of our hearts, and as a result, our lives feel void of vision.

When our lives are guided by our spiritual vision, we will be equipped to engage our destiny in God. Often, our true destiny seems very contrary to what we perceive in the natural. It may seem impossible or unlikely; we may feel unqualified or unable. These are our natural perceptions, based on insecurity and the critical environment of this world. If we make choices based on these perceptions, we will aim much lower than our God-given ability and calling. We will be prone to settling, thinking we can never be of much importance.

This, of course, is how we think after we grow up. Children do not think this way, which should clue us in to how God created us to think. Young children believe they can do nearly anything. If they want to be astronauts or doctors or teachers or the president, they believe they can do it. They often act out their destinies in their creative imaginary play. This is more than just imagination. It is a partnership with spiritual realities. Children have destiny seeds planted in their hearts from birth, and when raised in a healthy and empowering environment, they will begin to act out their destinies from a young age.

As a child, I loved playing I was a teacher and singer. In my mind, I saw myself singing and teaching in front of people, and as a result, most of my play time was spent acting out what I saw. In my childhood dining room, I would set up my audience of stuffed animals, grab a banana from the kitchen, and sing and teach. Though I did not know it was from God, from a very young age I perceived God's gifts and calling upon my life, which He had given to me before I was formed in my mother's womb (see Jer. 1:5).

I also saw this clearly in my oldest daughter, Danielle. From an early age, one of her greatest desires has been to be a mother. With a loving and compassionate heart, Danielle spent hours tenderly caring for her baby doll and her stuffed animals. In one of her preschool pictures, Danielle even posed holding her baby doll. To this day, Danielle speaks of her desire to become a mother. Some may assume this is typical of all girls, but it is not. Not all girls have the kind of vision for their future as a mother that Danielle does. Not all girls translate this compassionate mothering into every part of their lives in the way Danielle does. I know this because I have two daughters, and each of them is uniquely wired to pursue their destinies in different ways.

In Danielle, this mothering heart also manifests in a genuine care and concern for people. Because of this, Danielle earned a public and community service degree at college and is now pursuing her passion to care for those in need. She has given her time to many underprivileged people and worked in schools in a social-work capacity, giving freely of herself and her time. She has also traveled to other countries to help those who are less fortunate. In this way, her calling as one who nurtures and cares for those in need, not just for her own children but for all people, was acted out in her childhood play. Truly, destiny and purpose are locked up in what our children are captivated by.

As adults, we also can be in tune with our destinies, even if we are not yet walking in them. Joyce Meyer is an excellent example of this. For years she sensed her calling as an influential speaker and author, even though her reality seemed very far from that. As a mother raising her children and teaching a small Bible study, Joyce Meyer faithfully invested in her destiny by declaring what she saw in the spirit over herself. It would have been easy for her to assume she could never do what she dreamed of, based on her external circumstances or the likelihood of such a dream, but she didn't. Instead, she believed what God showed her in the spirit, and she regularly declared the truth of that spiritual vision over her life. Now, these years later, she is doing exactly what she saw in her heart.

Likewise, Joseph had a dream about his destiny that eventually came true, despite many circumstances that seemed to make that dream impossible (see Gen. 37). Unfortunately for Joseph, in his immaturity he did not keep his dream to himself, and his brothers hated and persecuted him because of it. From his experience we can learn about the importance of keeping some dreams hidden in our hearts until God tells us we can share them. Some people will not be able to understand the dreams God has put in our hearts, especially if they look at life only with their natural eyes. If we share these dreams with them prematurely, their criticism or mockery may make it harder for us to persevere in embracing the vision of God for our lives. Instead, like Mary the mother of Jesus, we must learn to treasure (hide and protect) in our hearts what God shows us about our destinies. *"But Mary treasured up all these things and pondered them in her heart"* (Luke 2:19).

Seeing by the spirit takes faith, because if we need to discern something by the spirit, it means it is not yet readily evident in the natural. For some of us, this feels scary. We have a hard time embracing and believing in dreams that seem so far outside our ability to make them happen. But this is exactly where we will find a vision of our destinies—when we stop seeing with our natural eyes and start looking in the spirit. When we see in the spirit, we will realize that anything is possible, and the physical hurdles that seem insurmountable are subject to the spiritual realities of God's power. Thus, we must ask God to enlighten the eyes of our understanding and to fill us with the knowledge of His will in all wisdom and spiritual understanding (see Eph. 1:18; Col. 1:9).

As we spend time in God's presence and train our minds and emotions to submit to the Spirit of God, we will begin to see with our spiritual eyes. He will show us things about our calling and about the future. He will enable us to perceive people and circumstances accurately. He will sharpen our vision so we can see with falcon clarity. Our destiny, which abides in eternity, is already written in our hearts. We just need to see it. As Ecclesiastes says, *"He has made everything beautiful in its time. He has also set eternity in the human heart"* (Eccles. 3:11). Within us live the seeds of destiny, planted by God. Whether or not they will ever bloom depends very much upon how we see and what we look at.

PRAYER OF REFLECTION

Father, give me spiritual understanding and wisdom to discern what is in Your heart and mind and in my own heart and mind. Enlighten the eyes of my heart; teach me to engage my ability to see with my spiritual eyes so that I will know who I really am, what I am called to do, and what is going on in the spiritual world all around me. I thank You, Father, that You have filled and equipped me with Your power so that I can live as an ambassador to this world without fear.

Chapter 3

---•---

HEARING WHAT'S COMING

What you see and what you hear depends a
great deal on where you are standing. It also
depends on what sort of person you are.
—C.S. LEWIS

On December 26, 2004, the deadliest tsunami in modern times rose out of the Indian Ocean, striking the shores of Indonesia, Sri Lanka, India, and several other nations—killing over 250,000 people and making more than a million people homeless. It was a tragic and horrific day! What makes a tsunami so dangerous is that it rises out of the ocean and crashes on the shore with very little warning. By the time people see the massive waves coming, they usually do not have time to flee to higher ground before they are overtaken by the quickly moving water.

In the days following the 2004 tsunami, some interesting reports regarding the animals in the affected areas began to surface. According to various reports, a large percentage of the animals (both wild and domestic) fled to higher ground—seemingly without explanation—just hours prior to the tsunami. As a result, very few animal deaths were reported. According to one wildlife expert, the reason for this is an ability many animals have to sense the approach of danger through changes in the environment:

> Earthquakes bring vibrational changes on land and in water while storms cause electromagnetic changes in the atmosphere. Some animals have acute sense of hearing and smell that allow them to determine something coming towards them long before humans might know that something is there.[3]

Some people refer to this ability in animals as a sixth sense. Other experts are skeptical about whether or not animals truly sense impending catastrophe, and for obvious reasons, solid evidence for the theory is difficult to come by. Regardless of whether or not animals actually possess this ability, the idea of a sixth sense in animals should cause us, as believers, to take notice. After all, if any creatures on the planet should have the ability to discern what's coming before it manifests in the natural, it should be spirit-filled believers in Jesus. In fact, the Bible tells us we have that ability because the Holy Spirit lives in us. Before He left earth, Jesus promised His followers:

> *But when he, the Spirit of truth, comes, he will guide you into all the truth. He will not speak on his own; he will speak only what he hears, and he will tell you what is yet to come* (John 16:13).

The Spirit came on the day of Pentecost (see Acts 2), and He has not left since. Because of His presence within us, we have the ability to perceive into the future, to hear the sound of what's coming before it hits the shore. The world and the New Age might refer to this ability as the sixth sense or divination, but it is simply the fruit of our relationship with our Father God. He loves us, and therefore He tells us about the future. He gives us promises of future blessings and also warns us about bad things so we can remain safe. As He did with the great prophet Moses, He now speaks with us face to face: *"The Lord would speak to Moses face to face, as one speaks to a friend"* (Exod. 33:11).

We find examples of this spiritual hearing or perception throughout Scripture. In the Old Testament, only certain individuals had close relationships with God and could hear His voice. (Now, all believers have His Spirit and can hear His voice—if they are listening.) Nehemiah, one of the blessed individuals who heard God speak in the Old Testament, was able to perceive the attacks of his enemy against him, which kept him from being deceived. When his enemies sent a false prophet to coerce Nehemiah to hide because of a supposed threat against his life, Nehemiah responded, *"Should a man like me run away? Or should someone like me go into the temple to save his life? I will not go"* (Neh. 6:11). Immediately afterward, Nehemiah perceived by the Spirit of God the true nature of the so-called prophet:

> *I realized that God had not sent him, but that he had prophesied against me because Tobiah and Sanballat had hired him. He had been hired to intimidate me so that I would commit a sin by doing this, and then they would give me a bad name to discredit me* (Nehemiah 6:12-13).

Here, as Nehemiah responded according to the courage God had given him to fulfill his calling to rebuild the walls of Jerusalem, God gave him supernatural understanding of the enemy's attempts against him. Similarly, when the psalmist Asaph felt discouraged and overwhelmed by the prosperity and success of wicked men, he found understanding and hope through listening in the Spirit. He wrote, *"When I pondered to understand this, it was troublesome in my sight until I came into the sanctuary of God; then I perceived their end"* (Ps. 73:16-17 NASB). Only in the sanctuary of God, where the presence of God dwelled during the old covenant, was Asaph able to gain understanding of the future.

In the New Testament, Jesus demonstrated a much greater and more consistent ability to perceive in the Spirit. Often, He responded to both His followers and antagonists based on what He perceived to be in their hearts or what He perceived in the situation (see Matt. 22:18; Mark 2:8; Luke 8:46; John 6:15). Not long after the feeding of the four thousand, Jesus perceived that His disciples were worried because they had forgotten to bring along bread on their journey. In His response, He connected a lack of perception with a hard heart:

> *Why are you talking about having no bread? Do you still not see or understand? Are your hearts hardened? Do you have eyes but fail to see, and ears but fail to hear? And don't you remember?* (Mark 8:17-18)

By mentioning hard hearts, Jesus referred back to a well-known prophecy in which Isaiah said God's people had lost their ability to see and hear in the spirit as a result of hardening their hearts against God. Thus, when Jesus came, many of them would not receive His offer of healing:

In them is fulfilled the prophecy of Isaiah: "You will be ever hearing but never understanding; you will be ever seeing but never perceiving. For this people's heart has become calloused; they hardly hear with their ears, and they have closed their eyes. Otherwise they might see with their eyes, hear with their ears, understand with their hearts and turn, and I would heal them" (Matthew 13:14-15).

Based on this, Jesus rebuked His disciples for having hard hearts instead of faith. This is the difference between those who are able to spiritually perceive and those who are not. The first are those with soft hearts of faith and trust toward God; the second are those whose hearts are hardened by sin and unbelief. In another place, Isaiah described this reality in the wicked, that though they experience God's blessing, the hardness of their hearts keeps them from perceiving the source of that blessing, and as a result, they do not turn to God: *"Though the wicked is shown favor, he does not learn righteousness; he deals unjustly in the land of uprightness, and does not perceive the majesty of the Lord"* (Isa. 26:10 NASB). By contrast, we who are filled with the Spirit of God are able to perceive present hidden realities and future realities when our ears are open and listening for the Spirit's voice.

After Jesus returned to Heaven and sent the Spirit to live in His followers, the early Church also demonstrated this ability to perceive by the Spirit (see Acts 10:34; 17:22; 23:6; 2 Cor. 7:8; Gal. 2:9). The two most notable stories of this ability to perceive, particularly related to the future, are found in Acts 11 and 27. In Acts 11, the prophet Agabus predicted a coming famine:

During this time some prophets came down from Jerusalem to Antioch. One of them, named

Agabus, stood up and through the Spirit predicted that a severe famine would spread over the entire Roman world. (This happened during the reign of Claudius.) The disciples, as each one was able, decided to provide help for the brothers and sisters living in Judea. This they did, sending their gift to the elders by Barnabas and Saul (Acts 11:27-30).

Because of Agabus' prophecy, the believers at Antioch (where this prophecy took place) were able to gather their resources and give gifts to provide for other believers in need. Because they could see what was coming, they were able to prepare appropriately so as not to be overcome by the difficulty.

Similarly, in Acts 27, when Paul was sailing to Rome to testify as a prisoner before Caesar, he perceived that the voyage would end in disaster and warned the centurion in charge: *"Men, I can see that our voyage is going to be disastrous and bring great loss to ship and cargo, and to our own lives also"* (Acts 27:10). But the centurion listened to the advice of the ship's captain instead, and they set sail against Paul's advice. Not long after they had set sail, they encountered such a great storm that all on board expected to lose their lives. Yet once again, Paul perceived what the outcome would be and was able to council the rest of the passengers:

Men, you should have taken my advice not to sail from Crete; then you would have spared yourselves this damage and loss. But now I urge you to keep up your courage, because not one of you will be lost; only the ship will be destroyed.... Nevertheless, we must run aground on some island (Acts 27:21-22,26).

This time, the centurion and captain listened to Paul and followed his directions, even destroying the lifeboat at his command (see Acts 27:31-32). As a result, as Paul predicted, the ship did run aground on an island, but all the people on board were saved.

This ability to sense what's coming by the Spirit is not reserved for super-spiritual Christians or leaders; it's a gift for all believers. However, it requires cultivation. As with spiritual sight, we are responsible to grow in our ability to hear in the spirit and discern the future. God usually does not force His messages on us. He speaks, and we get to chose whether we will be positioned to hear and obey. As we see in these verses from Isaiah, it is up to us whether we will pay attention and perceive what God is about to do:

> *Forget the former things; do not dwell on the past. See, I am doing a new thing! Now it springs up;* **do you not perceive it?** *I am making a way in the wilderness and streams in the wasteland* (Isaiah 43:18-19, emphasis added).

We cannot overestimate the importance of hearing in the Spirit. Of course, God is ever compassionate and patient with us. Because of this, sometimes He leads us despite our poor hearing. Often, we are led by the Spirit and don't even realize it until later (or perhaps we do not realize it at all). We are unconsciously led, which reminds me of a prophecy I heard from Kenneth E. Hagin once, that in the last days people would flow in the supernatural just as naturally as birds fly in the air and fish swim in the sea. While this can happen to us unconsciously, despite any poorness of hearing on our parts, our goal should always be to grow in our ability to hear what the Spirit is saying.

THE SOUND OF CHANGE

In our day, I believe this is especially important for leaders as we relate to the next generation. If we are going to relate to them in a way that is helpful, we must perceive the changes the Spirit has in store for the Church and the unique ways He wants to move in and through the next generation. It is so easy to become stuck in tradition—in the way things have been and the way we prefer—and to stop actively listening to hear what's coming next. However, if we want God to move in a greater dimension than He already is, we must be sensitive to what He is saying, and we must be willing to change. In Jesus' day, He accused the religious leaders of holding so tightly to their traditions that they made the Word of God of no effect (see Mark 7:13). We do not want to repeat their error.

The generation gap between many leaders in the Church and the youth and young adult generation is significant. If we want to keep the younger generation following after God, we need to be willing to make changes in our approach without compromising the unchanging message of the gospel. When we understand the times we live in, God will show us how to approach these times in a way that will advance His Kingdom (see 1 Chron. 12:32). If we are listening, the Spirit will show us how to maximize on the cultural changes happening around us and use them for His glory and the expansion of His Kingdom. For example, the younger generation does not watch TV nearly as much as they use the Internet. They don't listen to CDs; they listen to iTunes and podcasts. Because of this, I have tried to make as many of my materials as possible available on these venues.

Being aware of and embracing these simple changes will enable us to reach the younger generation more effectively.

But it will also require us to be willing to leave our comfort zones and try something new. God wants to shift us in our training and equipping methods for the next generation, and we as leaders need to hear what God is saying and what the youth need. Unfortunately, for many leaders it is hard to break out of our traditional comfort zones and do something new. But if we want to be effective, we need to stay relevant with the times without compromising our message. One idea God gave me was to begin recording fun, short vlogs, or video blogs, that I can post online. Often, while I'm about my day, God will give me a creative idea for a vlog, and I will record a two- or three-minute message or life lesson from the Word of God. Using my small Canon camera, I can do this wherever I am and immediately post it to various social media sites.

Considering that I did not grow up making and posting unedited videos of myself, recorded in my car or whatever random place I might be, it would have been easy for me to not follow through with this idea. But I am so thankful I did. God is very interested in reaching the youth, and it is though venues like social media and vlogs that they will hear our voices. Thus, when God pushes us to leave our comfort zones and try a new technique, we need to listen. The Bible says the one who wins souls is wise (see Prov. 11:30). The Spirit will give us wisdom in how to reach the younger generation, but we need to position ourselves to hear His voice and be willing to break out of our old patterns and into the new. Just as God told Moses to do things according to the pattern shown him (see Exod. 25:40), He wants to give us a pattern (or technique) for how to reach this generation. This is a very important part of the coming revival. The question is, will we listen for the sound of what's coming? And when we hear it, will we respond accordingly?

THE SOUND OF REVIVAL

God is not only speaking about changes needed to reach the next generation, but He is also speaking about how to prepare for the coming revival. Recently, while on a conference call with two pastor friends of mine, I shared with them the urgency I feel for the Body of Christ to gather together for corporate united prayer, specifically for our nation. As I was talking to them, I saw in my spirit a dark black cloud rolling into our nation. I knew the Lord was saying the strength of united prayer is what will push back the darkness developing in our nation, but if we don't pray, the darkness will overtake us. As a leader, it is my responsibility to share what I'm hearing and to sound a call to action so that we as the Church can respond accordingly. This is not just true for me but for all leaders in the Church, because God has appointed us as watchmen for His people.

Our ability to hear God's declarations about the future is important, not only for our own lives but also for the lives of people around us. What we perceive has the potential to greatly influence others and even to change history. This is the principle conveyed in God's warning to Israel about the need for faithful watchmen:

> *If the watchman sees the sword coming and does not blow the trumpet to warn the people and the sword comes and takes someone's life...I will hold the watchman accountable for their blood* (Ezekiel 33:6).

As those who hear in the Spirit, we are responsible to share what we are hearing and to teach others to cultivate their ability to hear as well. This is especially true for leaders, who are responsible to prepare the Church as a whole for the coming revival and expansion of God's Kingdom by helping believers mature and find where they fit in God's army. In an earthly army, the soldiers are assigned their position by their leaders, and they are led into battle by the sound of a particular trumpet or war cry. Paul used this metaphor to talk about our communication of what we hear in the Spirit when he wrote:

> *Even in the case of lifeless things that make sounds, such as the pipe or harp, how will anyone know what tune is being played unless there is a distinction in the notes? If the trumpet does not sound a clear call, who will get ready for battle?* (1 Corinthians 14:7-8)

In other words, we need to hear clearly so we can communicate clearly what is coming. Sadly, many prophetic voices in the Church today do not give a distinct sound that people can follow. The remedy for this indistinct sound is more time in the secret place of prayer. As a prophetic people, it is our job to spend time with God in the secret place of prayer. One of the results of this time spent with Him will be an understanding of *what is needed* in our times and *what needs to be done*. At times we need to teach, but at other times, teaching isn't what the Church as a whole or an individual church body needs. They may need revelation or prophetic insight so that a solution can be achieved. In order to discern what's needed and what we need to do, we must follow the anointing of the Holy Spirit. Only He is capable of guiding the Church.

On several different occasions, I have prepared beautiful sermon outlines, but when I stood up to speak, I found God wanted me to simply speak out of my spirit a prophetic message for that group of people. It takes faith to step out of our comfort zone (in this case my notes) and move into the realm of the unseen. I once heard Kenneth E. Hagin say that it isn't always easy following an unseen guide, but by faith, when we move with the anointing that flows from our hearts, we will be able to give the Body what is needed. This is what it takes to release a clear and certain sound, or battle cry.

In these days, it is vitally important that we do not give an uncertain sound; otherwise, the Body will not be prepared for the battles we face as we move into these last days. I have no doubt we are in the last days. We are living in uncertain times, but we have a God who, when we follow His voice, will guide us into victory at every step we take. Fivefold leaders are called to equip the Church for the great revival God wants to pour out in these last days, but if we don't follow the leading of the Spirit, the Church will be weak and unprepared. We are in a spiritual war, and we must focus on our goal so we can run the race to the finish line, without allowing distractions to hold us back. Not long ago, as I was speaking in a church in New York City, I saw a vision of a large train on the tracks, and I heard the sound of the engines starting. As I looked, the Lord said to me, "The train is already on the tracks, the engines have started, and the train is getting ready move." I believe the train symbolizes a powerful, fast-moving ministry or a powerful move of God. In other words, God is getting us ready for another major revival, and the time is very near.

Many prophetic voices have spoken about the coming revival in the last days—more than what I can share here. However, one word in particular has always stood out to me as a clear call regarding what's coming. Here, I will share a small portion of that word from Kenneth E. Hagin's book, *I Believe in Visions*. Hagin received this prophecy during a vision he had in 1950, when he was leading a tent meeting in Rockwall, Texas, at the age of thirty-three. During this vision, Jesus told Hagin this about the coming great revival:

All the gifts of the Spirit will be in operation in the Church in these last days, and the Church will do greater things than even the Early Church did. It will have greater power, signs, and wonders than were recorded in the Acts of the Apostles." He said that we have seen and experienced many healings, but we will now behold amazing miracles that have not been seen before. Jesus continued, "More and more miracles will be performed in the last days which are just ahead, for it is time for the gift of the working of miracles to be more in prominence. We now have entered into the era of the miraculous. Many of My own people will not accept the moving of My Spirit, and will turn back and will not be ready to meet Me at My coming. Many will be deceived by false prophets and miracles of satanic origin. But follow the Word of God, the Spirit of God, and Me, and you will not be deceived. I am gathering My own together and am preparing them, for the time is short.[4]

In this prophecy we see that the great revival of the last days is yet to come. Though the times may seem dark and difficult, revival is coming. A great outpouring of God's Spirit and the miraculous is coming, and we get to be part of it. This reality is what will motivate us to daily maintain our focus on the eternal realities of the Kingdom of God and what God wants to do on the earth through us. We simply need to hear the sound of what's coming and respond with focused obedience. This is true on a global level and also on a personal level. When each of us individually decides to live with focus on God's calling, the cumulative effect will have worldwide impact. The enemy would love nothing more than to distract us from our purpose and keep us focused on earthly things rather than the things of the Kingdom of God. But God has made us to be people who maintain laser-sharp focus, like the falcon—people who both hear and respond to the sound of what's coming.

PRAYER OF REFLECTION

Father, thank You for speaking clearly to Your people about what is to come. Give us ears to hear and hearts to listen so that we will be prepared for all You've placed before us. Teach me to step out of my comfort zone in response to Your guidance, and show me how You are calling me to prepare for the coming revival.

Chapter 4

---•---

ZOOMING IN

Lack of direction, not lack of time, is the
problem. We all have twenty-four-hour days.
—ZIG ZIGLAR

Now more than ever, developing our spiritual vision and perception is crucial to our destiny. Without it, we will not have a
clear sense of where we are going or what we are called to do.
However, it is only part of the puzzle. If we want our clarity of
vision and perception to bear fruit in our lives, we must also
have great focus. This is obvious if we think about the art of
photography, which relies heavily on the use of focus, not just
to clearly portray the subject of the photograph but also to
add meaning and visual impact. When a photographer zooms
in on an object, the photographer is able to see and capture
that object with greater clarity and detail. But a blurry picture
is ineffective and confusing.

My son, Jonathan, who is an excellent photographer, understands this concept of focus very well. Over the past few years, he has upgraded his lenses simply because he recognized the importance of having sharper and more accurate lenses that can focus very quickly and provide the best overall image quality. The same concept holds true in our lives. The sharper and more accurate our focus, the better the outcome of our lives will be. Vision without focus will be difficult to live by. Therefore, if we want to not only see in the spirit but also live according to what we see, we need to cultivate the discipline of focus in our lives.

Merriam-Webster's Dictionary defines focus, in part, as:

> a subject that is being discussed or studied, the subject on which people's attention is focused; a main purpose or interest; a point at which rays of light, heat, or sound meet.

Under a subcategory of one of the definitions of *focus* is this qualifying phrase: "adjustment for distinct vision." In other words, focus enables us to properly see the vision.

We see this principle in Scripture in the apostle Paul's summary of the Christian life: "*So we fix our eyes not on what is seen, but on what is unseen, since what is seen is temporary, but what is unseen is eternal*" (2 Cor. 4:18). Here, Paul makes a comparison between what we see with our natural eyes and what we see with our spiritual eyes. Both are seen, but only one should be the object of our focus. So, while we see both earthly and heavenly realities, our focus (our fixed gaze) must be upon the eternal realities we see with our spiritual eyes. We do not just look with our spiritual eyes; we also fix our gaze on what we see with our spiritual eyes. This is an important distinction, showing us the difference between vision and focus. We see many things, but we can only focus on a few. Focus is the difference between simply seeing and looking with intent.

Thus, in a very real way, we determine our experience in life through the realities we focus on. If, as Paul suggests, we focus on eternal realities, we will perceive a very different world from that perceived by those who focus on earthly realities. Winifred Gallagher, author of *Rapt: Attention and the Focused Life,* describes it this way:

> *The things that you don't attend to in a sense don't exist, at least for you.* All day long, you are selectively paying attention to something, and much more often than you may suspect, you can take charge of this process to good effect. Indeed, *your ability to focus on this and suppress that is the key to controlling your experience and, ultimately, your well-being.*[5]

Focus is what gives us the ability to place spiritual realities above earthly realities. It is also what gives us the ability to have faith in what God says to us, regardless of external circumstances. In the Book of Acts, we find an illustration of this in the life of Peter. Peter, as a senior apostle in the early Church, needed to have clear and focused vision for God's calling for his life and for the direction of the Church. During these formative years for the Church, Peter had a trance (an interactive vision) in which God revealed a drastic shift in priorities and beliefs regarding the Gentiles. Peter had spent his whole life being racist against the Gentiles, believing they were unclean and excluded from the people of God. This was a foundational belief of the Jews of his day; it's what helped them to keep themselves separate from the pagan cultures surrounding them. For Peter, stepping away from this belief required a huge shift in mindset. God knew this, and He gave Peter exactly what he needed so he could succeed.

Not only did God give Peter a vision showing that the old laws about clean and unclean no longer applied in the new covenant, but He also caused Peter's eyes to be fully fixed on the vision. By definition, a *trance* is a vision in which a person experiences a mental displacement, loses all awareness of the physical world around him, and is wholly fixed on the spiritual realities he is seeing.[6] When Peter later described this experience to the other apostles, he said, *"When I had fixed my gaze on it and was observing it"* (Acts 11:6 NASB). In other words, Peter's attention was fully fixed on the vision and trying to understand it, and as a result, God could reveal the meaning of it to him. Here, Peter's focus enabled him to understand and receive a direction from God that would have otherwise been difficult for him to accept. Thus, when the trance ended and Peter discovered three gentiles summoning him to the house of Cornelius, he was equipped with the wisdom to obey God's vision and share the gospel with the gentiles.

Likewise, when the prophet Ezekiel was taken by the Spirit of God in a vision to speak with an angel, the man told Ezekiel, *"Son of man, look with your eyes and hear with your ears, and fix your mind on everything I show you"* (Ezek. 40:4 NKJV). God needed Ezekiel to fully engage the message, not just seeing but also focusing on it intently. When God speaks to us, this is how He wants us to respond, too. He wants us to fix our minds on His vision and direction for our lives. When we do, we will be better able to run the race of our lives with perseverance. We will be more likely to succeed at what He has placed before us.

FOCUS FOR THE FINISH

Because focus enables us to see more clearly, it also enables us to pursue and fulfill the vision we are focused on. One aspect of *focus* is emphasis. When we focus on a thing, that thing receives greater attention and emphasis in our lives. Focus enables us to block out distractions so that we can look fully, with undivided attention. It is the posture described by David: *"My eyes are fixed on you, Sovereign Lord; in you I take refuge"* (Ps. 141:8), and by his wise son, Solomon: *"Let your eyes look straight ahead; fix your gaze directly before you"* (Prov. 4:25). What David and Solomon described is a sort of tunnel vision in which we look only at what is before us and ignore the surrounding objects in our peripheral vision. Obviously, this would not be ideal for our physical eyesight, but it can be very useful when it comes to the eyes of our hearts and our ability to focus on what God has put before us.

In a world full of distractions, the battle to avoid interruption and maintain focus is more intense than ever before. We face a constant barrage of emails, text messages, and social media interactions—not to mention needs and requests from other people. Never in history have people been so easily accessible; never has it been so difficult to hide away and focus for even an hour. Because of this, we all can learn from the example of the cheetah. Not only is the cheetah the world's fastest land animal (able to accelerate from zero to sixty miles per hour in only three seconds) but it also demonstrates amazing focus in pursuit of its prey.[7] What makes cheetahs such successful hunters is the combination of speed with laser focus and agility. They use their keen eyesight to pick out a prey, honing in on that one animal, and when the moment is right, they give chase. Because they pour all their energy into the hunt, refusing to be distracted by what's happening around them, they are able to strike with incredible speed and accuracy. Often, the chase lasts no more than a minute.[8]

Imagine what we could accomplish if we focused like that, pouring our best energy into the most important tasks before us. That is what God has made us to do. Contrary to popular belief, our minds actually are not made to multi-task. They are made to focus fully on one thing at a time, and they are far more efficient when they do.[9] However, talking about focus is a lot easier than making it a reality in our lives. So, for the remainder of the chapter, we will consider some practical tools for how to cultivate a life more focused on spiritual realities.

MAKING IT REAL

Not long ago, as I was spending time with the Lord, He spoke to me about the need for correct focus in the Church. He said, "Some people need to make a complete 180-degree turn to get back on track. Some need to turn around a quarter of the way and change their focus. Others just need a slight tilt of the head to get their eyes back on focus." In order to run this race successfully, some of us need to change our focus, and others of us need to cultivate a greater ability to focus.

Shifting Our Focus

If we are focused on anything other than knowing Jesus and living out His will for our lives, we need to change our focus. As members of God's family and ambassadors of His Kingdom, our minds and hearts must be fixed on Jesus. As the writer of Hebrews said, *"Therefore, holy brothers and sisters, who share in the heavenly calling, fix your thoughts on Jesus, whom we acknowledge as our apostle and high priest"* (Heb. 3:1). We cannot say we are engaging our heavenly calling if we are not fully focused on Jesus. The apostle Paul was such an example of a person focused solely on Christ and His Kingdom. He gave of himself fully in order to fulfill the call of God on his life, even when it required heartache, betrayal, persecution, and hardship. Paul was unflinching in his resolve; his eyes were always fixed on the eternal realities God had set before him, and he refused to turn aside:

> *Forgetting those things which are behind and reaching forward to those things which are ahead, I press toward the goal for the prize of the upward call of God in Christ Jesus* (Philippians 3:13-14 NKJV).

Like Paul and many Christian heroes who have gone before us, we must set our faces like flint toward the calling of God on our lives. Yes, as people who live on this earth, we should engage relationships and be faithful in our commitments. I am not advocating irresponsibility. But in all we do in our physical lives, our focus must always be heavenward, always asking, "How can I honor Jesus and fulfill His purpose for my life in this moment?" This sort of focus will enable us to walk the straight and narrow path Jesus talked about:

> *Enter through the narrow gate. For wide is the gate and broad is the road that leads to destruction, and many enter through it. But small is the gate and narrow the road that leads to life, and only a few find it* (Matthew 7:13-14).

In this passage, Jesus was speaking specifically in the context of eternal salvation. But the concept has a broader application. If we want to faithfully partner with God in the building of His Kingdom on earth, we may need to choose the road that may seem less popular. We may need to choose the narrow, tunnel-vision road in order to maintain our focus on Jesus. Such a road will help us follow the advice Joshua received just before he set out to fulfill his destiny by conquering the Promised Land:

> *Be strong and very courageous. Be careful to obey*
> *all the law my servant Moses gave you; do not turn*
> *from it to the right or to the left, that you may be*
> *successful wherever you go* (Joshua 1:7).

In this passage, we see that connected to the command to stay focused on God's will (not turning aside to the right or the left) is the promise of success in fulfilling our calling. This is so important for us to understand. Any goal or focus that does not come under our focus on Jesus will pull us from the narrow road and lead us into all kinds of distractions.

Cultivating the Focused Lifestyle

Once we have it settled that Jesus alone is the focus of our lives, we need to make practical decisions that align with our focus. The fact that in our hearts Jesus matters most does not mean we will not be easily distracted from His purposes for our lives. Some people think of focus as something that just happens in our lives if we're spiritual enough, but it's just not true. We all have the ability to focus and find great fulfillment when we are focused, yet our minds are prone to wandering and getting lost in lazy activities. Therefore, focus requires personal discipline. As Part 2 of this book demonstrates, many of us are easily (and often unknowingly) distracted, and we have lost focus. The question is, in the midst of the demands of daily life, how do we truly maintain focus?

According to Timothy Ferriss, best-selling author of *The 4-Hour Work Week*, "Focus is nothing more than eliminating distractions." He continues:

> Focus is a function, first and foremost, of limiting the number of options you give yourself for pro-crastinating.... I think that focus is thought of as this magical ability. It's not a magical ability. It's

put yourself in a padded room, with the problem that you need to work on, and shut the door. That's it. The degree to which you can replicate that, and systematize it, is the extent to which you will have focus.[10]

Ferriss' advice on focus is simple. We should use discipline and planning to minimize the opportunities for distraction and maximize our potential for focused work. So, for example, if we're trying to spend an hour in prayer, we shouldn't have our smart phone sitting right next to us, because the constant notifications will make it harder to maintain focus. Or, if we're working in a vocation or ministry God has called us to, we should guard our best hours, when we have the most energy, and give those hours to fulfilling that calling from God—not to less important tasks like checking email.

Eric Barker, blogger at the acclaimed *Barking Up the Wrong Tree* blog, lists five steps to increasing focus by increasing one's attention span.[11] Here are a few thoughts on how to begin applying these five steps in our Christian lives:

1. Reduce stress; it makes you frazzled and stupid.

In other words, too many commitments and responsibilities will weigh us down and keep us from giving our best to the things God has called us to. Also, a lack of intimacy in our relationship with God makes us prone to stress. Spending time with the Prince of Peace will enable us to experience the peace that passes understanding in our daily lives.

2. Give your best hours, when you have the most energy, to whatever is most important in your life.

Unfortunately, many of us have not objectively looked at our lives and asked, "What is really important, and what is not?" We should not be quick to commit to things outside our calling, no matter how good they may be, especially if they sap us of our ability to really focus on what God has called us to. It is true that the greatest enemy of "the best" is often "the good."

3. Dedicate specific blocks of time for important projects.

It may be a cliché, but it's true: Those who fail to plan, plan to fail. God doesn't just tell us our calling without giving us specific direction for how to move forward toward that calling. We simply need to listen for His direction and then be faithful in obeying, which often will look like intentionally scheduling time to work on the direction He's given us.

4. Do only one thing at a time.

As mentioned previously, multitasking makes us less effective and hinders our ability to truly focus. We must prioritize our time, giving our focus to one thing at a time, based on the priorities God has given us.

5. Practice meditation, which is weightlifting for your attention span.

Spending time with God builds our relationship with Him, and it also builds our ability to focus. It is spiritual nourishment and mental weightlifting all at once. The practice of being quiet and listening or praying in tongues for a certain period of time has the added benefit of training our brains to calm down and hone in on one thing—in this case, God. When we regularly practice prayer, not only will we grow in our relationship with God, but we will also grow in our ability to focus our minds on just one project. The benefit, as we've learned, is greater ability to perform at the level God created us to perform. Many of us are not using nearly the spiritual or mental capacity God has given us. Focus will help us perform at our best, which will make us much more likely to fulfill His plan for our lives.

These concepts are so simple, yet they are hard for many of us. We tend to spread ourselves thin and think the most spiritual thing is to serve as much as we can. While serving is incredibly important, it is possible to serve other people's callings to the detriment of our own. As with all things, balance is needed in the way we approach our time. Having clear focus will help. If we keep our eyes fixed on Jesus, know His priorities for our lives, and use practical tools to create a focused lifestyle, we will be well on our way to successfully fulfilling our calling in life.

PRAYER OF REFLECTION

Father, thank You for giving me a calling and purpose on this earth. Help me to live with Your will always in mind and to move purposefully toward it according to Your leadership. Please show me specific steps I can take to be more focused in my daily life and my calling. I want my eyes and heart to be fully fixed on You!

Chapter 5

---•---

RUNNING TO WIN

By perseverance the snail reached the ark.
—CHARLES H. SPURGEON

The Bible's primary example of the power of focus and perseverance is found in professional runners. In order to succeed, runners must block out all distractions from what's happening in their periphery and focus completely on the goal of finishing the race as quickly as possible. The best runners are not just physically fast; they are incredibly disciplined, and they know how to train their bodies and minds to fully focus on the race before them. Ryan Hall, a record-holding American marathon runner, is also a believer who trains to fulfill his God-given destiny. In a 2013 interview, Hall explained his running goals this way:

> I don't run for a paycheck, for fame, or to meet others' expectations. I run to test the limits of my

God-given ability and go after the dreams He has put in my heart—big dreams.[12]

This commitment to performing at his personal peak has caused him to train to push his personal limits—not just to do well. We could all learn from Hall's example. According to the apostle Paul, we, too, are runners in a spiritual race. He wrote to the early believers:

> *Do you not know that in a race all the runners run, but only one gets the prize? Run in such a way as to get the prize. Everyone who competes in the games goes into strict training. They do it to get a crown that will not last, but we do it to get a crown that will last forever. Therefore I do not run like someone running aimlessly; I do not fight like a boxer beating the air. No, I strike a blow to my body and make it my slave so that after I have preached to others, I myself will not be disqualified for the prize* (1 Corinthians 9:24-27).

Our race is not against other believers; it is a race to accomplish the tasks God has given us during our lives on earth. As with runners in the natural, focus is the key to success, the key to finishing our race without becoming weary or giving up. Considering that earthly runners cultivate disciplined and focused lives in order to win an earthly crown, how much more eager should we be to focus our lives in order to win an incorruptible crown? We are running our race for the glory of Heaven and the Kingdom of God, and all of Heaven—the great cloud of witnesses—is cheering us on.

> *Therefore then, since we are surrounded by so great a cloud of witnesses [who have borne testimony to the*

Truth], let us strip off and throw aside every encum-
brance (unnecessary weight) and that sin which so
readily (deftly and cleverly) clings to and entangles
us, and let us run with patient endurance and
steady and active persistence the appointed course of
the race that is set before us, looking away [from all
that will distract] to Jesus, Who is the Leader and
the Source of our faith [giving the first incentive for
our belief] and is also its Finisher [bringing it to
maturity and perfection]. He, for the joy [of obtain-
ing the prize] that was set before Him, endured the
cross, despising and ignoring the shame, and is
now seated at the right hand of the throne of God
(Hebrews 12:1-2 AMP).

Focus on God and His vision for our lives is what will enable us to throw off all the distractions that try to hinder us from running our race successfully. In the NIV, Hebrews 12 specifically highlights patience and the inward life as keys to running well: *"Let us run with perseverance the race marked out for us, fixing our eyes on Jesus, the pioneer and perfecter of faith."* In this final chapter of Part 1, we will consider two aspects of focus that will enable us to run the race of life well to the very end.

PATIENCE

Perseverance, or patience, is simply the ability to not give up when the race seems long. Impatience is rooted in self-will, while patience waits for God's will in God's timing. It is impossible for us to run our race with God while being impatient, because impatience will cause us to rush ahead of God. When, however, we abide in eternity, in our identity as sons and daughters of God, patience becomes our nature. After all, it is hard to be in a hurry when we have forever. So, we run to win, but only according to the leadership of our Father. Sometimes, when I consider all God has called me to do, I start to feel like, "God, when am I going to do this or that?" Then the Lord reminds me: "Just run with patience. Though the vision tarries, wait for it. I will speak, and it will surely come to pass." I'd rather be a little bit behind Jesus—and have Him as my focus—than be ahead of Him and not see Him anywhere.

Patience is really a matter of trust, and the truth is, we can trust Him. If we are faithful with what He has already given us, He will not forget us. He will fulfill the promises He has spoken over our lives. In Hebrews it says, *"God is not unjust; he will not forget your work and the love you have shown him as you have helped his people and continue to help them"* (Heb. 6:10). This promise of God's faithfulness to us is followed by a command to persevere in patience so that we will be able to run our races to completion and inherit all God has planned for us:

> *We want each of you to show this same diligence to the very end,* **so that** *what you hope for may be fully realized. We do not want you to become lazy, but to imitate those who through faith and patience inherit what has been promised* (Hebrews 6:11-12).

Here, the author of Hebrews tells us that belief in God's leadership, coupled with patience, will enable us to fulfill our destiny in Him. By contrast, trying to run on a path other than the one God has given us is a type of irresponsibility that is unwilling to wait on the promises of God. If we allow impatience to drive us, we will miss our purpose in the Lord. It is, by far, better to wait.

THE INWARD LIFE

The second principle for a focused and successful spiritual race mentioned in Hebrews 12 is cultivating the inward life: *"Let us run with perseverance the race marked out for us, fixing our eyes on Jesus, the pioneer and perfecter of faith"* (Heb. 12:1-2). In other words, our focus must not be merely on the tasks God has placed before us but on Jesus Himself. Ultimately, He is our goal. Communion with Him and the fulfillment of His will are the finish line we run toward. If our focus is on anything else, we will be prone to running according to our own strength and understanding and, as a result, missing out on God's will for our lives.

To fix our eyes on Jesus, we must do more than look for Him. We must look at Him. We must gaze into His eyes and give Him our full attention. We must run wholeheartedly toward Him as long-separated lovers run toward one another. One of the most profound examples of this in Scripture is Mary, the sister of Lazarus and Martha. The first time Mary is mentioned in Scripture, we find her acting against cultural norms to sit and listen as a disciple at Jesus' feet. The fact that this violated the expectations for what was appropriate for her as a woman in that culture shows us the desperation and hunger she felt toward Jesus. She didn't simply sit and listen because she had nothing else to do or because (as Martha suggested) she was too lazy to help in the kitchen. Mary must have known she would be criticized for her decision, but she did it anyway. She couldn't pass up the opportunity to sit and listen and look at Jesus. Nothing else mattered more.

Jesus recognized the heart motive of Mary's shocking decision, and when Martha accused her and demanded help from her, Jesus came to her defense:

"Martha, Martha," the Lord answered, "you are worried and upset about many things, but few things are needed—or indeed only one. Mary has chosen what is better, and it will not be taken away from her" (Luke 10:41-42).

What Mary had chosen—the better part—was the sort of intimacy with Jesus that we can only cultivate when we stop long enough to become still, to gaze into His eyes, and to listen to His words. Mike Bickle, founder of the International House of Prayer in Kansas City, often talks about the difference between being first a lover (like Mary) and being first a worker (like Martha). The reality is, both love and work are important to the Kingdom. We cannot run our race if we're unwilling to work, but what will give us the stamina and focus we need to complete our race is not hard work but deep love. Bickle points to Jesus' summary of the two greatest commandments:

"Love the Lord your God with all your heart and with all your soul and with all your mind." This is the first and greatest commandment. And the second is like it: "Love your neighbor as yourself" (Matthew 22:37-39).

The order of these commandments is important. First, we must love God with all we are; second, we must love and serve others. When we do these in the proper order, we will be lovers who can work untiringly because we are sustained by our intimacy with the Father. Thus, when we face hurdles in our race, we do not give up but are enabled to persevere because of the love of God in our hearts. Bickle explains it this way:

When we are lovers first, when the first commandment is first, our sacrifice and labor are rewarded.

This reward is twofold: (1) The Holy Spirit communicates to us that God loves us. (2) We become a vessel through which the Father's love for Jesus flows back to Him. This twofold reward keeps us invigorated, and therefore we avoid much of the burnout so common today...but we suffer greatly when we are workers first. When workers are mistreated, when the anointing of God does not show up as we want, or when circumstances disappoint us, we have nothing to fall back on—except waiting for heaven. The result of such pressure is usually burnout.[13]

This is the importance of the secret place for those who want to run their race to win. This has been an important revelation in my own life. I am the kind of person who likes to set goals and do projects. I find great fulfillment in getting things done. As a result, it is easy for me to rely on my own planning and my ability to accomplish. Sometimes, it is easy for me to forget that when I spend time with God I am making progress in developing intimacy with Him. It just doesn't seem as productive as checking items off a to-do list. Thus, in moments when I don't feel aware of what my prayer time is accomplishing, I need to walk by faith, believing that prayer is never a waste of time.

As I have learned to do this, I have discovered that when I put God first, the other things I need to do tend to come together more easily and are accomplished more quickly. The people I need to help me accomplish various projects and goals seem to just come into my life effortlessly. It is as though God is saying to me, "You prioritize spending time with Me, and I'll help you out with all the other things you need to accomplish." The impetus of our race must always be intimacy, not performance. When it is, we will find that the way we run when we're inspired by intimacy will always be superior to the way we run when we're driven to perform and work hard for God. As Bickle often says, "Lovers will always out-work workers." This is what Mary modeled for us.

At another time, after Mary had witnessed Jesus raising her brother Lazarus from the dead, she again prioritized intimacy and worshiped Jesus in a way that defied cultural norms and offended some of the people present.

> *Here a dinner was given in Jesus' honor. Martha served, while Lazarus was among those reclining at the table with him. Then Mary took about a pint of pure nard, an expensive perfume; she poured it on Jesus' feet and wiped his feet with her hair. And the house was filled with the fragrance of the perfume* (John 12:2-3).

While her brother sat with Jesus and her sister served Him, Mary took a large amount of expensive perfume and used it to anoint Jesus feet. When some of the people present criticized Mary's extravagant worship, saying the money could have been used to feed the poor, Jesus told them to leave her alone:

> *She has done a beautiful thing to me. The poor you will always have with you, and you can help them any time you want. But you will not always have me. She did what she could. She poured perfume on my body beforehand to prepare for my burial. Truly I tell you, wherever the gospel is preached throughout the world, what she has done will also be told, in memory of her* (Mark 14:6-9; see also John 12:7-8).

This is the value and priority God places on the secret place and our intimate relationship with Him. Though Mary was simply focused on expressing her devotion to Jesus, in her act of love she also unknowingly served Him by preparing His body for burial. Her great love for Him blinded her to all but Him. She was so focused on Him and her love for Him that she no longer cared what other people thought of her actions. As a result, her great love for Him positioned her to accomplish great things for Him. The same is true for each one of us. We will run a more focused and more successful race in this life when our eyes are fully fixed on Jesus and consumed with passion for Him.

Now that we have looked at the importance of spiritual vision and focus, in the second half of this book I will highlight ten lies that the enemy commonly uses to distract believers from the sort of focus we need in order to fulfill our destiny in God.

PRAYER OF REFLECTION

Father, I want to run my race to completion. I want to finish successfully and accomplish all You've destined me to do on this earth. Equip me with great focus for the finish line. Teach me to be patient. Remind me, when I forget, to make the secret place a priority in my life.

Part 2

---•---

TEN ENEMIES OF SPIRITUAL VISION

Chapter 6

———•———

OFFENSE

No one can make you feel inferior
without your consent.
—ELEANOR ROOSEVELT

Several years ago, when I printed my first prayer card to dis-
tribute to intercessors, God reminded me of the harm offense
can cause in our lives. Simply defined, *offense* is paying attention to unjust treatment from others or ways people have hurt
us in the past. *Offense* holds on to those hurts rather than letting them go. The prayer card had a prayer of commitment
to walk in love, and because I knew I needed love amplified
in my life, I decided to put the verses in the Amplified version. One day, though I had already read through it many
times, I read it again, and the Amplified translation of First
Corinthians 13 gripped me in a new way. The eyes of my
understanding were enlightened, as Paul talked about, and

I finally understood on a heart level the words I had read many times before. I saw the truth of it like I had never seen it before. That day, verse 5 seemed to jump out at me.

> *Love (God's love in us) does not insist on its own rights or its own way, for it is not self-seeking; it is not touchy or fretful or resentful; it takes no account of the evil done to it* [**it pays no attention to a suffered wrong**] (1 Corinthians 13:5 AMP).

As I read, the Lord said to me, "You are paying more attention to that person who hurt you and past offenses than you are to Me." In other words, I was looking at the offenses in my life instead of looking to Jesus, the author and finisher of my faith (see Heb. 12:1-2). Every time this person offended me, I kept looking at that person (instead of Jesus) and, as a result, I had lost my focus.

It is true that forgiveness comes by faith, not by feelings. However, if we are focused on the offense, even if our focus is for the purpose of forgiveness, we will have a hard time really letting go. What we focus on grips us. It holds our attention and informs our thought lives. Thus, the only way to let go of an offense is to focus on the one who makes forgiveness possible. What I learned about forgiveness that day was that it happens as we shift our focus from the offense and the offender to look at Christ. If we can keep our eyes on Jesus, we can walk in forgiveness. If we can train our spiritual eyes to be fixed on Him, we will not allow the hurts that others bring into our lives to distract us.

LOVING OUR ENEMIES

In my life, it often seems like at least one person is trying very hard to make life difficult for me. This is true for all of us. People who are not kind or encouraging regularly come into our lives. They rub us the wrong way, and if we don't deal with that rubbing, it can create a wound that gradually grows and becomes infected with bitterness. In this subtle way, offense can sink into our hearts and make us crippled on the inside. It can muddy the purity of heart Christ has given us and, if left there, can disqualify us from our purpose.

How sad it is when offense keeps us from destiny. In Christ, we are so much better than that. We do not need to sink into the pit of offense, because He has made us strong enough to climb many mountains. He has given us the spiritual vision we need to maintain focus on our goal, regardless of the dissenting voices and mean people who cross our paths. To do so, we must remember that some people will not understand us. Not everyone will appreciate us or believe the best about our hearts. Not everyone will accept the call of God on our lives. Others may even be offended at us, regardless of how kindly we treat them.

Some people are emotionally unhealthy and, therefore, easily offended. In this case, the issue is with them, not with us. Of course, we should always examine ourselves and make amends for any wrong on our end, but it is freeing to realize that sometimes, even when we do our best to live at peace with others, they will still be critical and harbor offenses toward us. This is why Paul added the disclaimer of sorts in Romans 12:18, *"If it is possible, as much as depends on you, live peaceably with all men"* (NKJV). Some people just do not want or know how to live at peace with others. When we encounter them, our job is simply to keep a clean slate and be resolute in love.

This is the kind of love Jesus was talking about when He said, *"Love your enemies and pray for those who persecute you"* (Matt. 5:44). Such love is the antidote for all offenses, because the love within us is greater than the hatred within the devil. The devil wants us to take hold of offenses, because he knows they will neutralize our impact, but when we follow Jesus' example and bless those who curse us, we will grow in spiritual authority (see Luke 6:28). Blessing those who hurt us does not mean we are affirming their choices. It means we are releasing to them a revelation of God's perfect love and unending grace. This is the power of love. So often, people who act in harmful ways do so because of various fears in their lives—fear of rejection, fear of losing control, fear of pain, and so forth. If we respond in kind, we only strengthen those fears in their hearts. But, if we learn to love our enemies, we invite them into a greater reality—that perfect love casts out fear.

As disciples of Jesus, spreading this revelation of love should be part of our life purpose. But if we are waylaid by offense in our hearts, we will not be able to do it. We will become just like everyone else, just like those who do not have the Spirit of God living in them, and we will sink below all that Christ died to give us. In Him, we truly can be free from offense and walk in perfect love, no matter the circumstances. But to do so, we must be willing to relinquish control.

RELEASING CONTROL

Our human desire for control can cause us to hold on to offense toward those who have hurt us, because we want justice for the wrong we suffered. This demand for justice makes it impossible for us to let go of the offense. Our desire to protect ourselves can also cause us to hold on to offense, when we say in our hearts, "I will never let someone do that to me again." Such a vow of self-preservation is an attempt to control the uncontrollable. We cannot prevent others from hurting us by controlling their actions. It simply isn't possible. Thus, attempts at control for self-preservation often lead people to protect themselves by shutting down their hearts and building large emotional walls. This, of course, only hurts the person, because we were not made for isolation.

The human dilemma of how to live in intimacy with others while protecting one's heart is solved in Christ. In Him, we find a third option. We do not need to let others hurt us, and we do not need to shut down our hearts to avoid hurt. Instead, when our hearts are protected by the love of Christ, we are able to have intimate relationships with others, and we are able to forgive the hurt that sometimes happens in those relationships. Only Christ has a love that is bigger and stronger than the pain of betrayal or persecution. The result of being grounded in His love is what I like to call "the ability to not take myself too seriously." When we take ourselves very seriously, we are very concerned with ourselves. We see every offense against us as a big deal. We demand justice and protection. This makes us easy to offend. It is a small and selfish way to live.

Jesus came and died to make us into mature people, those who do not need to get uptight about every little hurt and who know how to forgive the big ones. When our eyes are focused on Christ, we will not become so concerned with every offense against us. We will know that His love for us is enough; He is the one who proves our worth. He is the one who defends our reputation and rebukes injustice on our behalf. Letting go of offenses means releasing the need for control and self-preservation. It means choosing to believe and live like life is about more than us. When we do so, we will discover the power in Christ to live in love instead of fear. The more we live in God's love, the more offense-proof we will become. It doesn't mean people won't be able to hurt u,s but that when they do, we will be able to quickly release that hurt to our Father and find healing in His heart. We will be like waterproof phones.

Though we may get wet from time to time, the water will not damage us on the inside.

This is true humility, which Rick Warren has described like this: "True humility is not thinking less of yourself but thinking of yourself less."[14] In the Church, we often sing about wanting to know God's heart. Being free from offense is the key. If anyone would be justified in holding on to offense, it would be the perfect God, who has been repeatedly rejected and betrayed by His children. Yet God showed us the nature of love when He refused to harbor offense and instead forgave humanity in an act of radical love. He calls us to do the same: *"Bless those who persecute you; bless and do not curse"* (Rom. 12:14). What freedom comes from relinquishing control and fixing our eyes on Jesus! We cannot underestimate the power of living a life free of offense.

Finding Freedom

It doesn't matter what people have done. Freedom comes when we let it go. What many people fail to realize is that holding on to offenses always hurts us more than it hurts anyone else. Thankfully, we do not need to punish ourselves in the present moment because people hurt us in the past. Jesus has given us the power to overcome offense and to live in love, and He has promised to be our defender and to bring justice in our lives. This is what Paul wrote to the Romans about:

> *Do not take revenge, my dear friends, but leave room for God's wrath, for it is written: "It is mine to avenge; I will repay," says the Lord. On the contrary: "If your enemy is hungry, feed him; if he is thirsty, give him something to drink. In doing this, you will heap burning coals on his head." Do not be overcome by evil, but overcome evil with good* (Romans 12:19-21).

In the face of injustice, our job is always to act in the opposite spirit. We cannot overcome evil through retaliation. When the religious leaders accused Jesus of casting out demons by the power of Satan, Jesus said, *"Any kingdom divided against itself will be ruined, and a house divided against itself will fall"* (Luke 11:17). In other words, the problems people create when they hurt us cannot be solved through responding in kind. Sin cannot be cast out through sin, and pain cannot be healed through pain. The solution is found only in the opposite of sin and pain—the love of Christ. Evil is only ever overcome by the love of God. Love disarms the enemy.

Holding on to offense or lashing out in retaliation will not make people change. That is a lie the devil tells us, because he wants to keep Christ from being formed in us. He wants us to be controlled by the spirit of retaliation rather than the Holy Spirit. The truth is, only love can transform. When we are not consumed with our own importance, we will not retaliate. Instead, we will imitate Christ and lay down our rights for the cause of love. This laying down of our lives in love will release resurrection life into the situation. It will heap the burning coals of God's nonsensical love on those who have hurt us, and sometimes, they will turn and receive that love. Sometimes, through our refusal to hold on to offense, those who have hurt us may find healing. This is God's kind of justice. This is true freedom.

PRAYER OF REFLECTION

Father, I recognize the harm that holding on to offenses can cause in my life. Please open my eyes to see places where I have taken my focus from You and put it on the people who have hurt me. Help me to let go of those hurts and to turn my gaze back to You. I release every need for justice and control to You, and I ask for Your peace that passes all understanding. Help me to live an offense-free life and to follow Jesus' example of sacrificial love.

Chapter 7

―――――――•―――――――

PEOPLE-PLEASING

Anything you do because of political
pressures or opportunities will only lead
you to the end of your true ministry.
—RICK JOYNER

Many of us look to people for approval. To varying degrees,
we make decisions based on our desire to please people
instead of our desire to please God. One of the things God
had to burn out of my life is the fear of others' opinions.
Because I am such an introvert, for many years, when God
spoke to me about something He wanted me to address, it
was difficult for me to express those thoughts or opinions for
fear of being rejected. On top of that, as a woman in ministry in the early eighties, most of my peers were men. Today
women in leadership roles in the Church are very common
and widely accepted, but back then that was not the case. This
only added to my fear of speaking up.

For a season, I was on a board of a ministerial organization. The board was comprised of several men, the wife of the president of the organization, and me. At times, I had opinions to bring to the table, but I was afraid to share, because I was afraid I would not be taken seriously. Looking back, I now realize what I had to say was important to the team, and the president would not have asked me to serve on the board if he hadn't valued my opinion.

Years ago, at the church I was attending at the time, I received a specific word of knowledge in the form of a Scripture verse, Exodus 23:26. I instantly knew what the need was and that the Lord wanted to bring healing to this individual. I knew someone present wanted to have a baby but was having trouble conceiving and that God wanted to bring her the desire of her heart. I also knew that if I discreetly motioned to the pastor, he would allow me to give the word, and we would be able to pray for the woman. The people of that church knew me very well, and the pastor had given me freedom to operate in the revelation gifts. If I received any insight spiritually that would benefit the church, I had freedom to give it.

However, because I was afraid and feared people more than God, I sat in my seat and never gave that word. Even though this happened more than ten years ago, I remember the fear I felt so vividly. I remember the snare that kept me from meeting that woman's need. I also remember how I grieved the Holy Spirit and the hurt I felt in my heart over my decision to disobey God. Afterward, I vowed, to the best of my ability, to obey God whenever He moves in me. Thankfully, since then God has freed me from that fear of other people's opinions so that I can truly walk in obedience to the Lord's counsel.

As Proverbs 29:25 says, *"Fear of man will prove to be a snare, but whoever trusts in the Lord is kept safe."* The phrase *fear of man* refers to an anxious care about the opinions and actions of others.[15] It is commonly used to describe an attitude that can cause us to make choices based on expectations or pressure from others. It is the opposite of the fear or reverence of God, which causes us to prioritize His opinion in all we do.

The Hebrew word translated as *snare* in Proverbs 29:25 means "bait, lure, or snare."[16] In other words, people-pleasing is a dangerous trap. It will only lead us to heartache. But if we set our hearts on pleasing God, He will keep us safe. He is the only one who will never let us down. When we keep our eyes on Him, we are secure, and we discover who we really are.

FINDING OURSELVES

People-pleasers rarely know who they are or what they're made for. Because they're driven by the opinions of others, they have not valued discovering the gifts God has placed inside them. Unfortunately, we cannot depend on other people to value our uniqueness and abilities. We cannot depend on them to call forth the destiny in us. Some people will do so, but many will not. Only God knows the fullness of what we are made for, because He made us, and He longs to see us fulfill our purpose. While other people may try to use us for their own agendas, God empowers us to be more fully ourselves. He says, "You are amazing the way I made you, and I'm going to help you step into your destiny" (see Jer. 1:5).

When we look to God, we find approval. We discover His immense pleasure in us and love for us. His approval is what truly matters. Only God can show us our destiny and identity, and only in pleasing Him will we be able to step into it. When we keep our eyes on Him, our need for approval will be fulfilled in Him. As a result, we will be able to love people and walk in our destiny. We will live our lives from a place of emotional wholeness, because we will not be dependent on the ever-changing opinions of others.

Gideon discovered this truth when God found him hiding in his barn. Gideon was terrified of his enemies, the Midianites, but the angel of the Lord came to Gideon and told him who he really was, calling him a *"mighty warrior"* (Judg. 6:12). He told him he had within himself, by the power of God, what was needed to overcome the enemy. *"The Lord turned to him and said, 'Go in the strength you have and save Israel out of Midian's hand. Am I not sending you?'"* (Judg. 6:14). Gideon didn't even know who he was. He had no idea of the capability God had put within him, and he was too busy hiding in fear to figure it out. Only when he took his eyes off the threat of the enemy and focused on God's truth was Gideon able to rise out of fear of people and step into his destiny as a deliverer of Israel.

The same was true of Joshua. Joshua had spent his life in the shadow of the great leader Moses. When Moses died, Joshua assumed leadership of the nation. His first task was the conquest of the Promised Land. I'm sure, if Joshua compared himself to Moses, he found himself lacking. He wasn't the one who had spent forty days in the presence of God on Mount Sinai. He wasn't the one who had seen God face to face and lived to tell about it. We don't know what the Israelites thought about their new leader or whether people compared Joshua to Moses, but it is safe to guess that at least some people questioned whether Joshua would be able to fill his predecessor's shoes.

If Joshua had tried to meet his need for significance in the opinions of the people, he probably would have failed. But Joshua had a history of acting apart from the opinions of others. He had been one of only two spies (of the original twelve) who had believed God's pledge to give them the Promised Land, regardless of the giants they had seen there (see Num. 13-14). This experience had uniquely prepared Joshua to take Moses' place as one who looked to God, not the people, for his direction and affirmation. Immediately after Moses' death, God spoke to Joshua and gave him instructions for moving forward into the Promised Land. And He told him, *"No one will be able to stand against you all the days of your life. As I was with Moses, so I will be with you; I will never leave you nor forsake you"* (Josh. 1:5). For Joshua, this affirmation was enough to embolden him to lead Israel into a series of sometimes illogical battle moves—like marching around Jericho for seven days—that ultimately led to their conquest of the Promised Land.

In Joshua's example we see the absolute importance of being swayed by only God's opinion. Kathryn Kuhlman, the great faith healer, also recognized this reality. She once said, "If I had listened to my critics or my fans, I would have been quickly destroyed."[17] To this, Kenneth E. Hagin has added, "The mark of spiritual maturity is when criticism doesn't bother you, nor praise."[18] In other words, we are able to stay neutral, because our focus is Jesus. In my own journey toward freedom from people-pleasing, God once told me, "When you fear Me, you won't fear man."

The Bible often refers to fear of the Lord, not in the sense of terror but of awe and respect. When it comes to fear of people and fear of God, the question is: Who has the power to shape the course of our lives? Do we fear more the disapproval or disappointment of people—or of God? The person whose opinion matters most will most influence our decisions. Solomon, the wisest king in history, wrote: *"The fear* [reverential awe] *of the Lord is the beginning of knowledge, but fools despise wisdom and instruction"* (Prov. 1:7). If we want to be followers of Jesus, His opinion must matter to us more than any other. This is the beginning of wisdom.

We see the truth of this over and over in the stories of the Bible. The heroes of our faith succeeded where others failed (see Heb. 11), because they knew to focus on God's opinion and direction, not people's.

UNSHAKABLE CONFIDENCE

Jesus is our prime example of someone who was driven only by the opinion of His Father. Describing His ministry, He said, *"Very truly I tell you, the Son can do nothing by himself; he can do only what he sees his Father doing, because whatever the Father does the Son also does"* (John 5:19), and *"I do nothing on my own but speak just what the Father has taught me"* (John 8:28). Sometimes, what the Father led Jesus to do and say caused a lot of controversy. Many people loved Jesus, but many others hated Him and accused Him of heresy. More than once, crowds attempted to kill Him. But Jesus was not swayed by the opinions of the crowds or even of His own family members. He was guided only by the opinion of God, and that enabled Him to fulfill His destiny.

Once, Jesus asked His disciples, *"Who do people say the Son of Man is?"* (Matt. 16:13). He didn't ask this to boost His own ego but to gauge the perception of the crowds. Jesus already knew who He was and found full affirmation of His identity in God. He did not have a significance void He was trying to fill through public affirmation. Instead, Jesus was looking for a specific answer, and when Peter gave it to Him, Jesus affirmed him as having heard from God. This story shows us the secret behind Jesus' unshakable confidence, even in the face of criticism. He cared more about His reputation in Heaven than He did about His reputation on earth. He knew that what Heaven believed about Him was the truth, and if earth disagreed, earth was wrong.

After Jesus' resurrection, the disciples also began to walk in this confidence based on their identity in Heaven. We see this in the story of Peter and John's arrest after they healed the lame man at the Gate Beautiful. The religious leaders were confounded by what had happened. They knew they could not deny the miracle, but they thought they could silence Peter and John with threats:

Then they called them in again and commanded them not to speak or teach at all in the name of Jesus. But Peter and John replied, "Which is right in God's eyes: to listen to you, or to him? You be the judges! As for us, we cannot help speaking about what we have seen and heard" (Acts 4:18-20).

Because Peter and John had found their affirmation in Christ, they were unconcerned about the threats of the religious leaders. In fact, in response to these threats from the authorities, the apostles gathered together and prayed for greater boldness:

Now, Lord, look on their threats, and grant to Your servants that with all boldness they may speak Your word, by stretching out Your hand to heal, and that signs and wonders may be done through the name of Your holy Servant Jesus (Acts 4:29-30 NKJV).

Immediately afterward, the place where they were meeting was shaken by the Spirit, and they were all supernaturally empowered with greater boldness to speak and act according to God's will. This sort of confident reliance on God became a norm for the early believers, many of whom gave their lives for the gospel. The apostle Paul, one of the early church's greatest leaders, also modeled and defended the importance of valuing God's opinion over the opinions of people. Paul described himself as one appointed by God, not men: *"Paul, an apostle—sent not from men nor by a man, but by Jesus Christ and God the Father, who raised him from the dead"* (Gal. 1:1).

Thus, when God called him, Paul did not wait for approval from others. He simply obeyed God's word, even though I'm sure he knew not everyone would approve:

> *But when God, who set me apart from my mother's womb and called me by his grace, was pleased to reveal his Son in me so that I might preach him among the Gentiles, **my immediate response was not to consult any human being*** (Galatians 1:15-16).

When Paul heard from Heaven, he didn't look to people for approval. Paul lived with an unflinching commitment to looking to Jesus, regardless of what others might think. Of course, this does not mean he ignored the other apostles or refused counsel (see Gal. 2:9). Confirmation and support from other believers is an important safety net (see Prov. 11:14). We all have the potential to hear God wrongly. Paul did not overlook this truth. But he was so driven by the voice of God that he could not be swayed by opinions against what God had clearly spoken to him.

Thus, when even Peter and Barnabas were being racist toward the gentile believers, due to the influence of other Jewish believers, Paul called them to accountability. His conviction about the gospel of grace and the equality of all people caused him to confront Peter publicly, regardless of what people might say or do (see Gal. 2:11-21). The grace of the gospel was the message Paul had received directly from God, and he would not see it compromised. When he saw the people in the church of Galatia turning to people-pleasing, Paul rebuked them strongly, saying that following Jesus means giving up our desire to please people:

I am astonished that you are so quickly deserting the one who called you to live in the grace of Christ and are turning to a different gospel—which is really no gospel at all. Evidently some people are throwing you into confusion and are trying to pervert the gospel of Christ. But even if we or an angel from heaven should preach a gospel other than the one we preached to you, let them be under God's curse! As we have already said, so now I say again: If anybody is preaching to you a gospel other than what you accepted, let them be under God's curse! Am I now trying to win the approval of human beings, or of God? Or am I trying to please people? If I were still trying to please people, I would not be a servant of Christ (Galatians 1:6-10).

We cannot look to others for approval; only God can give us the affirmation we need to boldly hold to the truth and pursue our destiny in Him.

SEEKING GOD'S APPROVAL

Paul's advice to his spiritual son, Timothy, was to seek the approval of God, not people: *"Do your best to present yourself to God as one approved, a worker who does not need to be ashamed and who correctly handles the word of truth"* (2 Tim. 2:15). When we do this, our actions will be motivated by a desire to please God, and we will be diligent in all we do. Paul also highlighted this concept in relation to the way slaves related to their masters. The same could be applied today to the way employees relate to their employers. If we work with an eye to the opinion of God, we will always give our best, no matter who is watching.

Slaves, obey your earthly masters in everything; and do it, not only when their eye is on you and to curry their favor, but with sincerity of heart and reverence for the Lord. Whatever you do, work at it with all your heart, as working for the Lord, not for human masters, since you know that you will receive an inheritance from the Lord as a reward. It is the Lord Christ you are serving (Colossians 3:22-24).

If our actions are geared toward pleasing people, we will act inconsistently, based on who is watching. Only when our lives are guided by God's approval will we consistently live with integrity.

People who are driven by God's approval understand a very important biblical truth: Heaven is our real home (see Phil. 3:20). Everything we do should be informed by our value for and identity in Heaven. For me, this has been most applicable in my role as a mother. As all parents know, children are not always great at noticing and being thankful for all their parents do for them. It is simply a part of their growing-up experience. Sometimes, I struggled with that. I felt discouraged or frustrated by the lack of appreciation I was receiving from my kids. So I typed up Colossians 3:22-24 in the Amplified version of the Bible and hung it up around the house. I gave it a prominent spot in the laundry room and the kitchen to continually remind me to keep my focus. I wasn't being a good mother to get approval or praise from my children or other people. At the core, I needed to be doing it to please God. Only then could I truly love and serve them well, with an unselfish heart.

Really, that is the bottom line of finding our approval in God. Not only will we find the strength to do what He says, but we will be able to love and serve others wholeheartedly, without expectation of approval or praise from them. Yes, it is wonderful when people recognize how we serve and are grateful. That's how God intended human relationships to work. But He also knew they wouldn't always work that way. He knew people would sometimes overlook what we do or even try to manipulate us. When we work for the Lord's pleasure, we will be able to rise above both of these hurdles. We will not change what we do to perform for people, and we will not serve in order to be appreciated. Instead, we will simply obey the Lord, knowing we are laying up treasure in Heaven (see Matt. 6:19-20).

The Lord sees everything we do in secret, as well as the motives of our hearts. If we will allow it, the secret place of our hearts is where our true love and devotion can be sown, both to God and to those we serve. Our obedience pleases God and earns His approval; that is what matters most.

PRAYER OF REFLECTION

Father, I repent for all the times I've looked to other people's opinions instead of Yours. I'm sorry for valuing what people think above what You think. Shift my heart and the eyes of my spirit to focus solely on You. Remind me of the purpose for my life. You love and affirm me. Help me to never lose sight of that truth. I want to be driven by the desire to please You more than any other!

Chapter 8

———————◆———————

SELF-ABSORPTION

Embracing God's call is never easy, but
this is where the pursuit of a God-centered
life begins, and where the shame of
a self-centered life is exposed.
—COLIN S. SMITH

Growing up with five brothers, I was often teased. It was the Italian way of showing affection, but because of my melancholy and sensitive temperament, their teasing hurt me. I became really quiet and withdrawn, like a shrinking violet. Then, at the age of nineteen, I encountered God and He called me into ministry. To the shrinking-violet me, this was a terrifying prospect. But God told me, "I don't want you to look at your inadequacies. I want you to look to Me. I am the author and the finisher of your faith, and I will complete what I have begun in you." He was addressing my tendency toward self-absorption, toward continually looking at myself and my own weaknesses instead of looking to His strength. Thankfully, during my years at Rhema Bible Training College, I was able to learn to rely on God's adequacy instead of focusing on my own lack. Looking back, I realize how important that was. Had I focused on my own inadequacies, I never would have made it into the pulpit ministry God planned for me.

Apart from Christ, we all have the tendency to look to our own strength and assess it as either adequate or inadequate. Both are pitfalls for the Christian, because God calls us to do greater things than we could ever accomplish on our own. He calls us above and beyond ourselves in ways that require—if we want to be successful—dependence on His strength and power within us.

FOCUSING ON OUR WEAKNESS

I have always been more prone to focusing on my weakness in the face of a challenge. Many Christians see this attitude as a sort of humility because it recognizes human inability, but it is a false humility. Any focus on self, whether in a positive or negative light, is actually a form of pride. It makes the self bigger than God. It makes our inadequacies more potent than His strength and, as a result, chokes our faith.

Moses, in his early years, provides us with a textbook example of self-absorption. He was so focused on his own inadequacy that when God called to him from a burning bush, Moses nearly refused the call. In the face of such incredible supernatural power, he actually told God the mission would fail because of his own weaknesses. The problem is evident in Moses' objections: *"Who am I that I should go to Pharaoh and bring the Israelites out of Egypt? ...What if they do not believe me or listen to me and say, 'The Lord did not appear to* you'?" (Exod. 3:11, 4:1). Over and over, Moses says *"I"* and *"me"* without any reference to God's power. All he could see was himself. God, of course, was not at all worried about Moses' weaknesses, because He knew the mission wasn't dependent on Moses.

As God continued to push Moses to answer the call, Moses pointed out his inability as a speaker, as though that would be enough to hinder God:

> *Moses said to the Lord, "Pardon your servant, Lord. I have never been eloquent, neither in the past nor since you have spoken to your servant. I am slow of speech and tongue." The Lord said to him, "Who gave human beings their mouths? Who makes them deaf or mute? Who gives them sight or makes them blind? Is it not I, the Lord? Now go; I will help you speak and will teach you what to say"* (Exodus 4:10-12).

Here again, Moses' focus was completely on himself. In response, God reminded him who he was talking to—the Creator of Heaven and earth, the one who gave people the ability to speak in the first place. God was saying, "Sure, you may be a lousy speaker, but aren't you forgetting about Me? I invented speech, and I can handle this. You just need to trust Me." Because Moses was looking so intently at himself, he actually forgot the greatness of who God is and what He can do.

How self-absorbed does a person need to be to see such power and think his own weakness is great enough to cancel out the sufficiency of God? In effect, Moses was saying to God, "Though I see You can make a bush burn without being consumed, turn a staff into a snake, and heal leprosy, I do not think You are powerful enough to overcome my inability." It is an absurd idea, yet many of us can relate. Whatever we look at consumes our vision and becomes large in our eyes. In Moses' case, that caused him to doubt God's ability to use him.

What a crippling belief! The more self-absorbed we are, the more crippled we become. The truth is, Moses couldn't fulfill his destiny as the deliverer of Israel on his own. But, he wasn't on his own. God had promised to be with him and to help him. That was more than enough to make up for Moses' inability. Eventually, Moses learned to focus on God's ability as he faced the many daunting tasks before him. Over and over, he saw God come through for him. He experienced the reality the apostle Paul later described like this: *"By the grace of God I am what I am, and his grace to me was not without effect"* (1 Cor. 15:10).

Many of us can relate to Moses' struggle to accept God's call. We feel so aware of our own inability that sometimes it's all we can see. In those moments, we need the reminder Zerubbabel received from the prophet Zechariah:

> *"Not by might nor by power, but by my Spirit," says the Lord Almighty. "What are you, mighty moun-tain? Before Zerubbabel you will become level ground. Then he will bring out the capstone to shouts of 'God bless it! God bless it!'"* (Zechariah 4:6-7)

Zerubbabel, a descendant of the kings in David's line, but under Persian captivity, led the first group of Israelites back to Jerusalem. He had been commissioned by God and by the Persian king Cyrus to rebuild the temple, but the task seemed insurmountable. In the face of such a mountain, God reminded Zerubbabel not to look to his own strength but to rely on the strength of God's Spirit. No matter what each one of us faces, we can use the same reminder. Whether we feel capable or incapable of the task before us, the key to success is to take our eyes off ourselves and to focus on Jesus. Only His power within us is the hope of glory (see Col. 1:27).

He is the one who makes us sufficient for the task. When we give Him ourselves, no matter how weak we may be, He is capable of doing great things through us. When Moses gave God his shepherd's staff, he probably did not expect it to become the vehicle of a miracle. Yet God used that simple staff in many of the miracles He performed through Moses. The choice to look at God's strength instead of our weakness is an act of surrender. It is a statement of faith that God can do the impossible through us, that *"we have this treasure in jars of clay to show that this all-surpassing power is from God and not from us"* (2 Cor. 4:7).

FOCUSING ON OUR STRENGTH

The revelation of God's power at work in us is important, not only for those who see themselves as weak but also for those who see themselves as strong. To those of us prone to rush ahead in our own ability, Paul issued this warning: *"Do nothing out of selfish ambition or vain conceit"* (Phil. 2:3).

This, too, we can learn from the life of Moses, who made a tragic mistake that cost him the chance to enter the Promised Land. After more than forty years of relying on God's strength to lead the Israelites, Moses directly disobeyed a command from God. When the people needed water, God told Moses to command a rock to pour out water (see Num. 20:8). This was similar to something they had experienced before, when God told Moses to strike a rock to release a stream of water. This time, however, Moses did not follow God's instructions but simply did it the way he had done it before. He struck the rock instead of speaking to it (see Num. 20:11). Thus, he relied on his own strength and experience to create a miracle for Israel.

In the rebuke that followed, God attributed Moses' actions to a lack of trust in God (see Num. 20:12). In other words, Moses had taken his eyes off God's sufficiency and begun to believe in his own sufficiency. His foolish trust in his own ability led to the end of his leadership.

King Saul, the first king of Israel, also experienced the bitter result of self-reliance and self-absorption. Though he began his rulership in reliance on God, he quickly became prideful, because he attributed the exploits God did through him to his own greatness. As a result, he began leaning less and less on God's direction and more on his own abilities as a leader and warrior. The results were tragic for Saul and for Israel. Eventually, when Saul blatantly disregarded God's instructions in a battle against the Amalekites and then refused to repent, God rejected him as the king (see 1 Sam. 15). Though his reign continued on, Saul no longer had the Spirit of God upon him, and as a result he was tormented by evil spirits and lost many battles. It is a warning to us all of the danger in looking at the great things God does through us and seeing only ourselves and our own greatness. Though Saul had started out *"small in his own eyes"* (1 Sam. 15:17), he ended in arrogance.

In the examples of Moses, Saul, and many others, we find this truth: Our failures are the result of self-absorption, of looking to our own ability instead of God's. Instead, we must be like John the Baptist, who—when he encountered the greater ministry of Jesus—said, *"He must become greater; I must become less"* (John 3:30). When we keep our eyes fixed on His greatness—on His leadership and His strength in our lives—we cannot fail.

THE ADEQUACY OF CHRIST

In Christ we find our adequacy. Apart from Him, we will always be inadequate; apart from Him, we will always be unworthy of and ill-equipped for our destiny. He doesn't choose to use us because of our ability or worthiness but because of His great love for us as His children. He loves the joy of allowing us to partner with Him to accomplish far more than we ever could on our own. He is like the mother who enjoys baking cookies with her young child, even though the process takes longer and is much messier that way. The joy of doing it together and seeing the pleasure it brings her child is worth the extra hassle. In the same way, God enjoys working with and through us, but we should never imagine it's because of our own greatness or ability. It is only because of His goodness as a Father.

Because of His goodness, He has forgiven our sins and made us into new people who are filled with His Spirit. Now, regardless of what we lack in ourselves, we are empowered by His grace, and His supernatural life flows through us. It is the incredible mystery of the gospel, which Paul described this way:

> *I have been crucified with Christ and **I no longer live**, but Christ lives in me. The life I now live in the body, I live by faith in the Son of God, who loved me and gave himself for me* (Galatians 2:20).

Through Jesus' death and resurrection, the sufficiency of Christ has come to live within us and remake us into vessels of God's glory. This is the reality of our salvation. However, if we focus on ourselves and think our destiny is about what we can or cannot do on our own, we will miss out on that reality. We will sell ourselves short of the glorious truth of what Jesus has done for us. Instead, we must recognize that the same power that raised Christ from the dead now lives within us (see Rom. 8:11). We must recognize the ability (His ability) He has put within us and walk bravely into our destinies, not because we think we are able but because we know Christ in us is more than able.

Of course, the answer to a tendency toward self-absorption is not to try really hard not to focus on ourselves. It is, instead, to focus on what's in God's heart. What is His motive for the call He has put on our lives? The answer is simple: Love. Love is not self-seeking (see 1 Cor. 13:5). Our motive must always be love—love of God and love of others. After all, God has empowered us so that we may release His love to the world. Boiled down, that is His mission for all of us. We are carriers of His love who get to meet the needs of the people around us through the supernatural ability of Christ living in us.

This is a foolproof test of our focus on God. Are we compelled by love to meet the needs of others? The apostle John said it this way: *"And so we know and rely on the love God has for us. God is love. Whoever lives in love lives in God, and God in them"* (1 John 4:16). The Christ in us is driven to meet the needs of others in love. When we focus on God, we will be focused on love. We will stop thinking so much about ourselves and willingly pour ourselves out as an expression of God's love to the world.

PRAYER OF REFLECTION

Father, I am sorry for the times I have seen my own inability or ability as being more potent than Your divine ability at work in my life. Help me to not make excuses about what I am not good at or to rush ahead of Your leading, thinking I can manage on my own strength. Instead, I want my vision to be consumed with Your ability to achieve any task. I want to always be obedient to Your calling.

Chapter 9

---•---

FOCUS ON THE PAST

Yesterday is gone. Tomorrow has not yet
come. We have only today. Let us begin.
—MOTHER TERESA

Looking to the past will keep us from reaching our destiny in the future. This is one of the primary distractions the enemy uses against God's children to keep us from seeing life with God's spiritual vision. He loves to remind us of the ways we have failed or others have failed us in the past. He taunts us with these failures and suggests our future will be full of more of the same. If we believe him, we will live as emotional and spiritual cripples. We will take our eyes from the possibilities and promises of God's vision for our lives, and we will embrace hopelessness. This is not God's plan for us. We see this in Jesus' statement: *"No one who puts a hand to the plow and looks back is fit for service in the kingdom of God"* (Luke 9:62). If we are looking backward, we will be unable to walk forward. We won't be able to live in the freedom Jesus died to give us.

For this reason, we all need to make the choice to let go of the past and any regret or shame associated with it. Only we can do that for ourselves. This choice comes down to one question: *Who will we believe?* Will we believe the enemy's lies, when he tells us our past defines our future? Or will we believe the promise of God to make all things new in our lives? The choice is up to us. When we stand before God in Heaven, only we will be responsible for that choice and whose voice we decided to believe. Let's make the right choice and, like the apostle Paul, refuse to focus on the past:

> *But one thing I do: Forgetting what is behind and straining toward what is ahead, I press on toward the goal to win the prize for which God has called me heavenward in Christ Jesus* (Philippians 3:13-14).

Paul had a darker past than many of us. Before he encountered Jesus, He arrogantly and aggressively persecuted God's people. He even watched with approval as people killed the first Christian martyr, Stephen (see Acts 7-8:3). But when Jesus stepped into his life and made him into a new creation, Paul decided to believe God's promise that his past would not hinder his future. Each one of us can do the same.

LOST OR FAILED RELATIONSHIPS

For many of us, the most painful aspects of our past lives relate to lost or failed relationships—the death of loved ones, divorce or breakup, betrayal from close friends, or alienation from family members. These events cause great pain in our hearts. They often cause us to ask why and sometimes to pass out blame. In my own life, I experienced an unexpected and painful betrayal from a close friend and ministry partner that taught me the importance of not only forgiving but also moving on.

God often uses me to strengthen and confirm callings on individuals. This is how I met my friend, who was a member at a church I often ministered at. Though she was not in full-time ministry at the time, she was being groomed for ministry, and I was part of the grooming process. As the years passed, we also became very close friends, and we spent a lot of time encouraging one another in the things of God. When I entered into a new phase of ministry, I asked her to be one of the people on my team who would remain close to the ministry as an advisor and give input in the decision-making process.

Then, one day I received a typed letter from her stating her resignation from my team. Among other things, she said she was going to another level in God and I was not on the same level as her. She also rebuked me, saying I had missed the leading of the Holy Spirit at a conference we had both attended. I was shocked—not only by her resignation but also by the way she had attacked me personally. Until that moment, I had no idea she was not committed to me as a friend and co-laborer in ministry. Though her choices hurt me deeply, I chose to forgive her and to move on, not only in my ministry but also in my heart.

While it is very important to grieve relationship losses, it is also important to eventually let go so we can continue on with our lives. This is the pattern God gives us, as illustrated in the story of the death of Moses. His death was a significant loss for the children of Israel, especially as they faced the conquest of the Promised Land. Many must have wondered how they could continue on without him. After all, it was Moses who, at God's leading, had united them and freed them from Egypt.

He had led them through the wilderness and mediated a covenant with the God of their ancestors. I'm sure many of them felt lost without him. Had they embraced that feeling of loss, they may have stayed where they were forever. But God gave them a limited mourning period before they needed to continue moving toward their destiny in the Promised Land.

After the prescribed thirty days of mourning had passed, God spoke to Joshua, the nation's new leader: *"Moses my servant is dead. Now then, you and all these people, get ready to cross the Jordan River into the land I am about to give to them—to the Israelites"* (Josh. 1:2). It was time for them to get back up and keep moving forward. The same applies to us. When we experience loss in our relationships, God gives us a grace period for mourning. But eventually, He tells us it's time to rise up and move ahead into a new place. It's time for the next leg of our journey, but if we hold on to the losses of the past, we will not be able to fully engage the present. That weight will keep us from fully focusing on the race ahead.

Imagine what would have happened if the Israelites had begun comparing Joshua to Moses and complaining about how things were different now than they used to be. Such discord could have divided the nation and caused them to miss out on the Promised Land. That's what looking to the past with regret will do in our lives, too. Continuing to mourn the loss of what was and refusing to let go will keep us from our full potential in Christ. God doesn't want us to get stuck in grief but to find healing in Him and the strength to move on to new things.

When King Saul betrayed Samuel's trust and turned away from God, Samuel was grieved. However, God had a new plan. The loss of King Saul had not compromised His ability to place a righteous ruler over His people. So, He told Samuel:

*How long will you mourn for Saul, since I have
rejected him as king over Israel? Fill your horn with
oil and be on your way; I am sending you to Jesse of
Bethlehem. I have chosen one of his sons to be king*
(1 Samuel 16:1).

In other words, God was telling Samuel, "Don't hang on to
your desire for Saul to be a righteous king. I've moved on, and
so should you." Sometimes, we are tempted to cling to relationships that have died, in hopes of resurrection, when God
is telling us it's time to move on. Our personal destiny will
not be limited or destroyed by the loss of relationships in our
lives. We are the only ones who have the power to destroy our
destiny. Loss may cause a rerouting of the path to our destiny,
but the Holy Spirit is our perfect guide. If we refuse to cling
to the past, He will guide us toward a magnificent future. It is
like the biblical metaphor of the potter and the clay. *"But the
pot he was shaping from the clay was marred in his hands; so the potter formed it into another pot, shaping it as seemed best to him"* (Jer.
18:4). Loss sometimes requires a change, a reshaping process.
When that happens, we can trust our Potter to remake us into
an even more beautiful pot.

When the early Church experienced the loss of members,
the apostle John counseled the remaining believers:

*They went out from us, but they did not really belong
to us. For if they had belonged to us, they would
have remained with us; but their going showed that
none of them belonged to us* (1 John 2:19).

Those who left were not tied to the destiny or success of
the group as a whole. In fact, as this passage seems to indicate, sometimes people leave because they are not helpful
to our destiny. We may not be able to recognize the purpose
in it, because of the pain of the loss, but we can trust that

God knows what is best for us. Sometimes He leads people out of our lives for this very reason. At other times, people who should have stayed close have chosen to leave on their own, and we have suffered because of it. Yet, we can find comfort in the fact that their choices cannot sabotage our destiny. God's plan is always bigger. All He needs from us is a willingness to turn our eyes from the past to look toward the future.

PAST SIN AND FAILURE

The same applies to our mistakes and failures in the past. The enemy loves to remind us of our sin and the ways we have disappointed ourselves and others. He loves to drag the past into the present. By contrast, God forgives our past and sees us according to the perfect nature of Christ. Paul explained this reality this way: *"Godly sorrow brings repentance that leads to salvation and leaves no regret, but worldly sorrow brings death"* (2 Cor. 7:10). God's conviction of sin in our lives causes us to repent and receive His forgiveness, which leaves us with *no regret!* That is a powerful statement: No matter what we have done, God's forgiveness can free us of all regret.

If we continue to experience regret, it is a clue that we are not experiencing conviction from God but condemnation from Satan. This is the worldly sorrow that brings death. Satan wants us to kill our dreams and destiny through regret, but God removes our transgressions from us *"as far as the east is from the west"* (Ps. 103:12). In doing so, He makes us new creations in Christ who are no longer defined or limited by our past sins. *"Therefore, if anyone is in Christ, the new creation has come: The old has gone, the new is here!"* (2 Cor. 5:17). In Christ, old things pass away, and all things become new. This is not just true at the moment of salvation but every day thereafter. He forgives us and makes us new *daily*.

When we live with humility and are quick to repent, the mistakes of yesterday stay in yesterday. As the writer of Hebrews said:

Let us then approach God's throne of grace with confidence, so that we may receive mercy and find grace to help us in our time of need (Hebrews 4:16).

When we humbly run to Him for forgiveness, instead of hiding in pride, not only will He have mercy on us, but He will give us more grace to overcome. Paul said it this way: *"Where sin increased, grace increased all the more"* (Rom. 5:20). That, of course, does not mean it's good to sin but that His grace—His divine empowerment—is always sufficient to overcome the sin in our lives. The key ingredient is humility. Because, *"God opposes the proud but shows favor to the humble.' Humble yourselves, therefore, under God's mighty hand, that he may lift you up in due time"* (1 Pet. 5:5-6). What a glorious promise—that when we humble ourselves in repentance, He will lift us up. He does not keep reminding us of the past but, instead, brings us into newness of life and guides us toward our destiny. When we really believe this, we will stop focusing on our past sins and failures and truly trust God's mercy and grace.

The truth is, it takes more courage and faith to get up and move on from the past than it does to wallow in self-pity, regret, and failure. No matter what we have done, when we come to Jesus, the past is a canceled check. Jesus has forgiven it; our job is to rip it up and allow our hearts to move on. If we do not forgive ourselves, as Jesus has forgiven us, we will sabotage our destiny just like Judas. Peter and Judas both betrayed Jesus, but they responded to the guilt of that betrayal differently. Judas hanged himself. Despite traveling and ministering with Jesus for three years, Judas felt no hope for forgiveness in his life, so he ended it. Peter also experienced great guilt and shame over his betrayal, but when Jesus offered him forgiveness, Peter accepted it. As hard as it may have been, he chose to accept Jesus' new evaluation of him—not as a fickle disciple but as a leading apostle of His new Church (see John 21:15-17).

We cannot change where we have been or what we have done in the past, but we can determine where we are going. We can decide whether we will be like Judas or like Peter— whether we will trust in the forgiveness of Christ enough to let go of the past. His eyes are always toward our future, His arms always pulling us forward into our potential.

AUTHOR AND FINISHER

This is why the Bible refers to Jesus as both the author and the finisher of our faith. He authored our faith by dying on the cross and forgiving our sins, and He completes or perfects our faith by guiding us toward the fulfillment of His plans for our lives. He is the one who does it, not us. As Paul joyfully declared:

> *I am convinced and sure of this very thing, that He Who began a good work in you will continue until the day of Jesus Christ [right up to the time of His return], developing [that good work] and perfecting and **bringing it to full completion** in you* (Philippians 1:6 AMP).

We cannot complete our faith by our good works, and we cannot hinder it by our failures. Instead, we are fully dependent on His mercy to forgive and His grace that empowers us to live righteously. Yes, we partner with Him through believing His promises, but on our own, we are incapable of bringing His good work into fruition in our lives. The other side of that reality is that our sins and failures in the past cannot hinder His ability to work in our future, as long as we are humble before Him. When we understand that, we will be able to shake off the negatives in our past and run our race with perseverance:

> *Therefore, since we are surrounded by such a great cloud of witnesses, let us throw off everything that hinders and the sin that so easily entangles. And let us run with perseverance the race marked out for us, fixing our eyes on Jesus, the pioneer and perfecter of faith* (Hebrews 12:1-2).

As someone once said, "Winners never quit, and quitters never win." To succeed in God, we just need to keep moving forward with Him, to keep trusting His goodness and ability in our lives. Focusing on the past will handicap our ability to do that, but looking to the future and all God has ordained for us will give us the courage and strength to keep persisting, even in the midst of difficulty. Forward vision strengthens us, while looking backward weakens our resolve. This simple truth is what sets apart those who succeed in life and fulfill their destiny in God. In life, we all make mistakes and fail at times; we all have painful experiences. This is a common denominator throughout humanity. What sets some of us apart from others is how we chose to respond to our failures and the hurts of life. To succeed in life, we must take our focus from the past, forgive ourselves and others, and look with hope toward the future.

PRAYER OF REFLECTION

> *I am so thankful, Father, that my past does not define my future. Today, I choose to let go of lost relationships, sins, and failures in the past, and I*

choose to look forward at the destiny You've called me to. By Your grace, the pain of the past cannot harm my future. Help me to fully release the past to You and move forward, trusting in Your forgiveness and grace.

Chapter 10

THE EASY ROAD

Many people are defeated
by secondary success.
—HARRY TRUMAN

If you only do what is easy, you
will always remain weak.
—JOYCE MEYER

We live in a culture obsessed with the easy life. We accumulate labor-saving devices, electronic gadgets, and packaged food in an effort to make our lives easier and more enjoyable, yet many Americans are not very happy at all. Making our lives easy has not actually made them more enjoyable. In fact, recent studies seem to indicate that the happiness factor in life comes more from the experience of pursuit than from the ability to sit back and relax.[19] The easy life is not all it's thought to be. An important factor in pleasure is working hard to pursue a dream.

This applies even more to the Christian life, in which God has given each one of us destiny dreams and goals to work toward. He does this not only because He wants us involved in the work of the Kingdom, but also because He knows that a lifestyle of pursuing dreams is actually pleasurable for us. That's how He made us to live—always progressing forward and overcoming obstacles in order to achieve greatness. Yes, we find our joy in His presence. He is our ultimate source of pleasure, yet part of our pleasure in Him is pursuing who He made us to be and the dreams He put in our hearts. This is why the appeal of the easy road is such a devastating lie.

If we believe the easy road holds more fulfillment and pleasure than the challenging road, we will be tempted to settle for lesser purposes instead of pursuing the fullness of our destiny. As the saying goes, "Good is the enemy of best." If we are not focused on God's plans for our lives, the good things in life can distract us from the best things. God's highest and best for our lives is not an easy or quick accomplishment. If it was, we wouldn't need His help. Instead, His best for us requires hard work, commitment, and perseverance. Many of us don't want to hear this, but it's the truth. The high road may not be easy, but if we are willing to take it, we will discover it is the best.

AN ATTACK ON DESTINY

The temptation to settle for an easier way is really an attack on our destiny. It is the lure to exchange maximum potential for an easier road. However, God does not call us to do small things. He often calls us to accomplish more than we can imagine—and along the way, we often encounter much adversity. Certainly, some of the difficulties in life are caused by our own poor decisions and immaturities. But many of the conflicts we experience are a result of what we are doing right, not what we are doing wrong.

When the enemy sees us advancing with our focus locked on the plan of God, he works very hard to distract us from that goal through adversity and confusion. He adamantly opposes the destiny on our lives. When we experience opposition, it is a good time to ask ourselves, "What is my calling? What is the anointing on my life and the fullness of who God has made me to be?" Whatever that is for each one of us, that is what the enemy is trying to steal. That is the area of our lives where he will try to introduce doubt, confusion, and sin to distract us from our potential. The struggles we face are in proportion to our calling.

We should not be surprised by this. When we read the Bible and look at the lives of the heroes of our faith, we have no reason to expect the easy road. All of us experience spiritual warfare that opposes the work God has given us. Even the great apostle Paul faced great opposition (see 2 Cor. 6:4-10). He said of his ministry, *"A great door for effective work has opened to me, and there are many who oppose me"* (1 Cor. 16:9). This is a normal part of the Christian life.

We are in a battle, and if we are not facing difficulty, we need to ask ourselves why. In the natural world, soldiers expect to encounter adversity. They prepare for a fight. The same should be true of us in the spirit realm. We are at war with the spiritual forces of darkness, and as a result we will experience attack from our enemy as we pursue our calling. The good news is, the enemy does not have the power to overcome us as long as our eyes are fixed on Christ. Paul, who experienced much persecution, wrote:

No temptation has overtaken you except what is common to mankind. And God is faithful; he will not let you be tempted beyond what you can bear. But when you are tempted, he will also provide a way out so that you can endure it (1 Corinthians 10:13).

God always provides a way out, a counterattack or rescue mission that enables us to stay on the path toward our destiny, no matter what the enemy throws at us. He also rewards us for our perseverance. He is so proud of us when we do not allow the enemy's tactics to drag us down or distract us from the mission before us:

Blessed is the one who perseveres under trial because, having stood the test, that person will receive the crown of life that the Lord has promised to those who love him (James 1:12).

In the midst of adversity, He gives us the crown of life so that we can prosper emotionally and spiritually. He makes a beautiful way in the wilderness. In this way, though we encounter difficulty in pursuing His best for our lives, we also encounter the greatest reward and blessing. Nothing is more fulfilling than walking step by step with the Father and experiencing His peace and joy that surpass our understanding.

A LESSER REWARD

The story of Moses gives us an example of this. Though Moses was adopted into the royal family of Egypt, with wealth and opportunity at his fingertips, he left it all to pursue God's call:

By faith Moses, when he had grown up, refused to be known as the son of Pharaoh's daughter. He chose to be mistreated along with the people of God rather than to enjoy the fleeting pleasures of sin. He regarded disgrace for the sake of Christ as of greater value than the treasures of Egypt, because he was looking ahead to his reward (Hebrews 11:24-26).

He chose destiny over the fleeting pleasures of sin, and as a result he fulfilled his destiny as the deliverer of Israel. This was not an easy task. It would have been so much easier to enjoy his position in the royal family while his people suffered in slavery. Thankfully, Moses did not choose the easy road. He did not value the rewards of earth but the rewards of Heaven. Because his eyes were fixed upon obedience to his destiny, he rejected earthly sonship and kingship in order to gain a heavenly reward. He realized any earthly riches and fame would be a lesser reward compared to the joy of fulfilling God's call. As a result, though outwardly Moses faced much difficulty in his life, he experienced great intimacy with God. Not only was he known as the most humble man alive, but he was the only one God spoke to face to face (see Exod. 33:11; Num. 12:3). The prize of intimacy with God trumps all others, which is why Moses later pled with God: *"If your Presence does not go with us, do not send us up from here"* (Exod. 33:15).

Many other heroes in the Bible made great sacrifices and faced great difficulty because of their pursuit of God's call on their lives. Daniel refused to eat the king's food, though it would have been much easier than bucking the system (see Dan. 1:8). But eventually, his counter-cultural decisions led him to a place of influence in a pagan kingdom. Certainly, it would have been easier for Joseph to simply go along with Potiphar's wife's attempts to seduce him than to face imprisonment, but Joseph chose the harder road (see Gen. 39). As a result, after years in the prison, Joseph miraculously became second-in-command of the nation. The easy road is not always sinful, but it does always mean settling for less than God's best. It means receiving a lesser reward.

Even secular people recognize the value of overcoming adversity as we work toward our goals. In every area of life, those who reach the greatest heights are the ones who have had the greatest training—not just in education but in overcoming adversity and failure. Malcolm Gladwell's book, *David and Goliath,* speaks to this reality and the benefit that people sometimes incur from being underdogs who have to fight harder than everyone else to succeed. Good parents recognize the truth of this in parenting. If we don't allow our children to face adversity and figure out how to overcome it, they will be handicapped as adults, because life is full of adversity. The question is this: Will we use the adversity in our lives as a learning tool as we pursue destiny, or will we allow adversity to derail us from our destiny?

Having it easy should not be our goal. If our lives are easy, it simply means we are settling for less. Instead, our goal should be to accept and overcome the challenges we face on the way toward fulfilling our destiny. The greatest generals in history are those who won the most desperate battles. In this moment in history, we are invited to become great generals in God's army who will fight willingly and bravely the battles before us.

TRUE HAPPINESS

The amazing thing about the harder road is that, in God, it is where we will find true happiness. I have experienced this in my own life many times. In the early eighties, God called me to pioneer a prayer movement on the East Coast, which certainly was not the easy road. I worked hard teaching and motivating the Church to hear the call to prayer, both secret prayer and corporate prayer. God also called me to gather leaders from a region and host corporate prayer meetings in a neutral place. I did this in multiple cities along the East Coast. This was before the prayer movements we know about today, and many Christians had no grid for a lifestyle of prayer or how to pray for more than fifteen minutes at a time. Not only that, but I was the first woman to preach or teach in many of the churches I visited.

Being a pioneer is never easy. The early settlers in America didn't move here for the easy life. They moved here to pursue their dreams, recognizing that shaping those dreams out of the wilderness would be both difficult and rewarding. In the same way, we pursue happiness in our lives by following God when He calls us to blaze a trail and trusting Him when the going is tough. Sure, it's easier to stay home, to cultivate a social life and accumulate possessions, or to do whatever else we think might make us happy, but those things will never truly satisfy. The easy road cannot possibly fulfill us when we are called to labor in love for God's Kingdom. Discipline, determination, and focus will pay off when we are working with God for His Kingdom. But recognizing this on the front end requires a change in our paradigm. As New York City pastor Joseph Mattera says:

> As believers, our value system should not be based on a temporal paradigm (view) of materialism and earthly significance but on an eternal paradigm based on faith and obedience to the Lord Jesus Christ.[20]

When our value system prioritizes faith and obedience over pleasure, we will discover true happiness in the journey with God, no matter what it entails. It was true for me in the eighties, and it is true for me now.

During my years of pioneering, I have faced a lot of turbulence, but God always strengthens me and gives me the grace I need to blaze new trails for Him. Looking back on my season of pioneering in the eighties, I can see the amazing fruit of that prayer ministry, not only in my life but in the lives of many churches and people. That reward is worth the struggle I experienced in those years laboring as a pioneer of the prayer movement. The same is true of my life now, as I pursue the dreams and visions God has placed before me in this season. The same can be true for all of us. When we reject the lie of the easy road and listen to God's invitation to come higher and to pursue greater things for His glory, the difficulties we encounter will be far outweighed by the pleasure of partnering with God and seeing His Kingdom come on earth. That is true happiness.

PRAYER OF REFLECTION

Father, I repent for the times I have wanted the easy road instead of Your high calling. I pray that You would strengthen my heart and give me the courage to face adversity for the sake of my calling and Your Kingdom. I thank You that true joy and fulfillment are not found on the easy road but on the path You've chosen for me. I ask that Your Spirit would lead, guide, and direct all of my decisions. I choose to follow Your leading and do my best to follow You, not the dictates of my soulish nature.

Chapter 11

---•---

THE NOISE OF THE ENEMY

Satan knows that if he can defeat us in our
mind, he can defeat us in our experience.
That's why it is so important that we not
lose heart, grow weary and faint.
—JOYCE MEYER

Two weeks out of each calendar year, I teach in an international Bible school that trains leaders from all around the world. Recently, during one of those weeks, beginning on the first day of class, I began to have nagging thoughts. It was really soft and subtle—a fiery dart here and a fiery dart there—until I found myself feeling very aggravated. But I had no idea why. *What is bothering me?* I wondered. Thoughts of discouragement and thoughts that the work of God I was doing was bearing no fruit bombarded me. As these thoughts started to slip into my mind, I even began to feel physically tired and emotionally drained. I wasn't the only one feeling this way. I could discern a heaviness over the entire classroom, but I didn't do anything about it. I just tolerated those negative thoughts for a whole day.

By the next day, the thoughts were stronger, and finally I said, "What is this, Lord?"

"You're being distracted," He said.

"By what?" I asked.

"The noise of the enemy. He's speaking at you in your mind, and it's distracting you. He's trying to get you off course, trying to get you to lose your focus. What is your purpose for being here? I want you to stay fully engaged in this assignment and to fully equip these students. But the devil's trying to distract you."

In Kenneth E. Hagin's book, *I Believe in Visions,* he tells a story of a time when he was distracted from hearing the voice of Jesus because of the noise of the enemy. One night, in 1952, Hagin had a vision in which Jesus appeared to him and began to teach him many things about spiritual warfare. Then this happened:

> While Jesus was talking to me, an evil spirit that looked like a monkey ran between Jesus and me and spread out something that looked like a black cloud or a smoke screen. I couldn't see Jesus anymore. Then the demon began jumping up and down, waving his arms and legs, and yelling in a shrill voice, "Yakety-yak, yakety-yak, yakety-yak." I paused for a moment. I could hear the voice of Jesus as He continued to talk to me, but I could not understand the words. I thought to myself, *Doesn't the Lord know I am missing what He is saying? I need to get that—it is important—but I am missing it.*

I wondered why Jesus didn't command the evil spirit to stop. I waited for a few more moments. Jesus continued talking as if He didn't even know the evil spirit was present. I wondered why the Lord didn't cast him out, but He didn't. Finally, in desperation, I pointed my finger at the evil spirit and said, "I command you to be quiet in the Name of Jesus Christ!" He stopped immediately and fell to the floor. The black smoke screen disappeared and I could see Jesus once again. The spirit lay on the floor whimpering and whining like a whipped pup. I said, "Not only must you be quiet, but get up and get out of here!" He got up and ran away. I was still wondering why Jesus had not stopped this evil spirit from interfering, and of course Jesus knew what I was thinking. He said, "If you hadn't done something about that, I couldn't have." "Lord, I know I misunderstood You! You said You couldn't do anything about it, but You really meant that You wouldn't." "No," He said, "if you hadn't done something about that spirit, I couldn't have."[21]

In these stories we see the reality that the enemy often tries to distract us from hearing God's voice by making lots of noise.

WARFARE IN OUR MINDS

The Bible tells us the devil is *"the accuser of our brothers and sisters"* (Rev. 12:10). He loves to sneak into our thoughts and plant accusations against others and even against our own selves in our minds. See, not all the thoughts we think are our own thoughts. Sometimes they are lies the enemy whispers in our ears, and they enter our minds disguised as thoughts from our own souls. While our focus must always be on Jesus, we also must be aware of the devil's schemes against us so we can silence his noise (see 2 Cor. 2:11). If we don't realize what is going on and address it, this noise from the enemy can be incredibly distracting to our purpose and goals. The psalmist described this reality when he wrote:

> *[I am distracted] at the noise of the enemy, because of the oppression and threats of the wicked; for they would cast trouble upon me, and in wrath they would persecute me* (Psalm 55:3 AMP).

Athletes have difficulty focusing and performing well if too much noise and distraction is bombarding them. Such excellence requires extreme focus. That is why, in basketball, fans for the opposing team often try to distract or heckle players while they're taking free throws. If they can successfully get in a player's head and cause distraction, the player is much more likely to miss the shot. This is exactly what Satan tries to do. He stands behind the basket, jumping around making all the noise he can while we take our shot. The more successful he is at distracting us and causing us to miss the basket, the more he will continue. Fortunately, once we recognize the source of the noise, silencing him is simple.

It's not always easy to discern which thoughts are ours and which ones come from the devil. Here are a few tests I rely on to help me discern the source of the thoughts in my head:

1. *Does it line up with the Word of God? Is this what God says about me in His Word?* God's voice will never contradict the Bible.

2. *Does it make sense practically?* Sometimes the enemy speaks accusing thoughts against others that are completely illogical or counterintuitive.

3. *Do I feel peace in my heart? Or do I feel fearful and anxious?* God's voice is always accompanied by an inner peace.

4. *Does it bring condemnation or pressure?* God's voice brings conviction, not condemnation, and He never pressures us. He is both patient and kind.

5. *Does it grieve my spirit? Do I feel darkness or heaviness?* Our spirits quickly discern the source of the thoughts in our heads, because our spirits are tuned to the Holy Spirit.

6. *Is it a half-truth, but twisted in a way that does not convey God's heart?* Sometimes the enemy will speak facts in a way that contradicts God's heart. He is a master at taking the Scripture out of context.

7. *Does it bring confusion or disharmony? Is it bringing accusation against someone I have relationship with?* God always desires to bring clarity and unity and to strengthen and heal relationships.

These sorts of questions uncover the distinct sound of the devil's voice. He loves division, accusation, and confusion. He enjoys distorting the facts and encouraging us toward wrong conclusions about ourselves and others.

This sort of mental warfare distracts us because it causes us to listen to or look at negatives (whether fact or fiction) instead of the Lord's promises. God always comes to us with encouragement and strength, but the enemy seeks to introduce doubt and fear. The Bible paints a stark contrast between the intentions of God and the devil. In this contrast, we discover the sounds of their voices:

For I know the thoughts and plans that I have for you, says the Lord, thoughts and plans for welfare and peace and not for evil, to give you hope in your final outcome (Jeremiah 29:11 AMP).

The thief comes only to steal and kill and destroy; I have come that they may have life, and have it to the full (John 10:10).

While the enemy plots all kinds of evil against us, God works only for our good. Thus, we can discern the source of the thoughts in our minds by analyzing their intent and fruit. The enemy sends thoughts of evil—any thoughts that would tear down our confidence in God and our hope for our lives, ministries, or vocations. This why it is so important to be rooted and grounded in the Word of God (see Matt. 7:24-25). When we know what God's Word says about us and His plans for us, we will be able to quickly recognize any thoughts that do not align with it. But if we don't know what the Bible says, we may be easily deceived.

In Joyce Meyer's excellent book *Battlefield of the Mind,* she talks about how the enemy uses distracting and confusing thoughts as spiritual warfare against us. She says, to combat the enemy's noise our minds must be deeply convinced of the love of God for us. When that is the case, we will be so rooted in His love and truth that the enemy's lies will not be able to shake us. She says:

I had an unconscious, vague sort of understanding that God loved me, but the love of God is meant to be a powerful force in our lives, one that will take us through even the most difficult trials into victory.[22]

Thankfully, God has given us a simple tool for dealing with distractions—the name of Jesus. His name is the ultimate weapon of our warfare:

> *For though we live in the world, we do not wage war as the world does. The weapons we fight with are not the weapons of the world. On the contrary, they have divine power to demolish strongholds* (2 Corinthians 10:3-4).

Our weapons are not of the physical realm, but the spiritual realm, and they are so much more powerful than any weapon fashioned by human hands. When God spoke to me about the enemy's attempts to distract the Bible school students and me through accusing thoughts, I was grieved in my spirit. I went to class the next day and took authority over the enemy on their behalf and for myself. I stood up in front of the class and corporately commanded accusation to go in the name of Jesus, and just like that, it lifted. It really is that simple, because in the name of Jesus we can make demons leave (see Mark 16:17). As James promised us: *"Submit yourselves, then, to God. Resist the devil, and he will flee from you"* (James 4:7). We can tell accusing and distracting thoughts from the enemy to be silent in the name of Jesus, and they must obey.

To silence the enemy's lies, we also must speak the truth of God's Word aloud in order to cast down deceiving thoughts and imaginations. I find that every time God gives me a new assignment or I go into a new level of influence, I experience an increase in warfare. For example, two weeks before the launch of our first Kingdom Intercessors United (KIU), I experienced very intense warfare. I could sense the enemy, but I did not allow him to overtake me. Every morning when I woke up, the first thoughts that would come to my mind were, *What are you doing? Who do you think you are? Don't expect*

God to be with you in this meeting. In response, I would momentarily pull the covers up over my head, but then I would throw them off and declare, "I can do all things through Christ who strengthens me! It's not my vision; it's God's vision!" I would speak the Word to the enemy, purposefully deciding not to allow the warfare to stop the prayer movement. I knew the warfare would pass as soon as KIU had successfully launched.

As this story shows, we must provide the truth to counter the enemy's lies. Jesus did this when the devil tempted Him in the wilderness (see Luke 4:1-13). No matter what the devil said to Him, Jesus always referred back to the truth of God's Word, saying *"It is written."* In this way, He defeated the enemy. Paul also emphasized the power of the Word of God as a spiritual weapon against the noise of the enemy:

> *Put on the full armor of God, so that you can take your stand against the devil's schemes. For our struggle is not against flesh and blood, but against the rulers, against the authorities, against the powers of this dark world and against the spiritual forces of evil in the heavenly realms. Therefore put on the full armor of God, so that when the day of evil comes, you may be able to stand your ground, and after you have done everything, to stand. Stand firm then, with the belt of truth buckled around your waist, with the breastplate of righteousness in place, and with your feet fitted with the readiness that comes from the gospel of peace. In addition to all this, take up the shield of faith, with which you can extinguish all the flaming arrows of the evil one. Take the helmet of salvation and **the sword of the Spirit, which is the word of God** (Ephesians 6:11-17).*

The Word of God, which testifies to the truth about Jesus, is the only offensive weapon on the list above. The armor protects us, while the Word of God enables us to advance against and gain victory over the lies of the enemy. This is so important to understand. Many believers are not strong in their knowledge of the Bible, and as a result, when they hear distracting and accusing thoughts, they do not know how to combat them with the truth.

WARFARE IN OUR RELATIONSHIPS

Not only does the enemy try to get into our minds and distract us from God's vision for our lives, but he also sometimes uses the people around us to attack our destiny. This is a different sort of warfare, because it is not within us but around us—often coming from people we know and love. When God is calling us to co-laborer in building His Kingdom and take risks in faith, not everyone will understand or appreciate our choices. Then, sometimes, like the psalmist, we experience the pain of betrayal: *"Even my close friend, someone I trusted, one who shared my bread, has turned against me"* (Ps. 41:9). Like Joseph, we get to forgive when our family and friends turn on us because of the call of God on our lives (see Gen. 37:5-36).

Jesus also knew what this was like. At the beginning of His ministry, many of His family and the people He'd grown up with in His hometown were offended at Him when He began to travel, teach, and perform miracles:

> *Coming to his hometown, he began teaching the people in their synagogue, and they were amazed. "Where did this man get this wisdom and these miraculous powers?" they asked. "Isn't this the carpenter's son? Isn't his mother's name Mary, and aren't his brothers James, Joseph, Simon and Judas? Aren't all his*

sisters with us? Where then did this man get all these things?" And they took offense at him. But Jesus said to them, "A prophet is not without honor except in his own town and in his own home." And he did not do many miracles there because of their lack of faith (Matthew 13:54-58).

While we might think His friends would have been the quickest to support Him and believe His message, the opposite was true. However, He had the support of His mother, Mary, who had also learned to stay focused on the will of God, despite what others thought. When as a young and unmarried woman she became pregnant with the Son of God, she must have known most people would not be able to believe what had happened to her. So, *"Mary treasured up all these things and pondered them in her heart"* (Luke 2:19). She kept the precious revelation God had given her safe in her heart, sharing it only with a few people, like her cousin Elizabeth. When God is doing new things in us, our friends and family may not be able to accept it. At those times, like Mary, we should use discernment about who is ready to hear our treasure. This will help protect our hearts from spiritual warfare through our relationships.

Another woman named Mary also encountered warfare from her family because of her choice to prioritize her devotion to Jesus above social expectations. When Jesus came to her house, Mary sat at His feet and listened (with the men) instead of helping her sister Martha in the kitchen. Martha became so frustrated with Mary that she actually asked Jesus to rebuke Mary on her behalf. But Jesus did just the opposite. He commended Mary for her choice and allowed her to position herself as a disciple, even though it was unacceptable in their culture (see Luke 10:38-42). Though Mary was vindicated in the end, she had to make an offensive decision and face persecution from her own family for her choice to follow Jesus so radically.

Jesus also experienced betrayal from friends at the end of His life. Not only did one of His closest friends turn Him over to the authorities, but the rest of His friends ran away when He was arrested. No one stood with Him as He walked that final leg of the journey toward His destiny, but Jesus did not allow that to keep Him from obedience to His Father's will. He knew that the joy of the victory over sin and death would be worth the suffering He endured (see Heb. 12:2).

The same is true for us when we persevere in the face of betrayal or persecution from our family and friends. When those we love oppose or ridicule or punish us for our decision to pursue the call of God on our lives, we can remember the promises of Jesus:

> *Blessed are those who are persecuted because of righteousness, for theirs is the kingdom of heaven. Blessed are you when people insult you, persecute you and falsely say all kinds of evil against you because of me. Rejoice and be glad, because great is your reward in heaven, for in the same way they persecuted the prophets who were before you* (Matthew 5:10-12).

> *No one who has left home or brothers or sisters or mother or father or children or fields for me and the gospel will fail to receive a hundred times as much in this present age: homes, brothers, sisters, mothers, children and fields—along with persecutions—and in the age to come eternal life* (Mark 10:29-30).

Being misunderstood by close friends and family can hurt our hearts. We long for the support of those we love as we step out in faith toward our destiny. When people disappoint us in this, it is important to remember the spiritual realities behind what we're experiencing. Our friends and family are not our enemies. They just do not understand, or they have rejected God's will. But our true enemy is the devil, who deceives and brings accusation into relationships in an attempt to get us to forfeit our destiny. Seeing that he is the source of the persecution we face helps us persevere and push forward with even more tenacity. The truth is, he can only overcome us if we allow him to distract us from our focus on God's call. But if we stay the course, his warfare against us will only make us stronger. We will be like the Israelites: *"The more they were oppressed, the more they multiplied and spread; so the Egyptians came to dread the Israelites"* (Exod. 1:12). Even the enemy's attacks against us, when we face them with the right attitude, can move us toward our destiny.

PRAYER OF REFLECTION

Lord, give me the wisdom to recognize the warfare against my destiny—both in the thoughts that enter my mind and in opposition from friends and family. I resist any thoughts that are not from You. Train me in discerning the difference and quickly silencing the noise of the enemy. Also, give me the courage I need to obey Your voice when others criticize or persecute me for it. I want Your strategies for how to love and honor them while resolutely following Your leading.

Chapter 12

---•---

DISCOURAGEMENT

Successful people in every field are those
who refuse to be stopped, even though
they don't see the fulfillment of the promise.
You are not going where you are going
without problems—no one does. The world
is not fair, so do not be surprised when you
are not treated fairly. Every bad thing that
happens to you can either make you bitter or
make you better. Bitter people never win.

—RICK JOYNER

When Peter and the other disciples saw Jesus walking toward them across the stormy lake, they were terrified, thinking He was a ghost. But Jesus said, *"Take courage! It is I. Don't be afraid."* In response, Peter said to Jesus, *"Lord, if it's you, tell me to come to you on the water."* When Jesus told him to come, Peter stepped out of the boat and began to walk atop the waves. Yet despite this miracle, Peter quickly lost his focus and allowed the threat of the wind and waves to take away his courage. As he did, he began to sink. Jesus, of course, lifted Peter back up and helped him to the boat, and He rebuked him for his lack of faith (see Matthew 14:22-32).

What happened to Peter is a common scenario for many of us. The tumult around him distracted him from his focus on Jesus, and as a result he became discouraged. He allowed his circumstances to determine his courage and resolve for his future, instead of relying only on what Jesus had said—*"Come!"* Courage is what we need to hold on to in the situations of life. But courage is fed by vision, and when we lose our vision, we can quickly become discouraged. For this reason, our vision—our forward-looking hope—is one of our most valuable possessions. Through discouragement, the enemy seeks to destroy our vision by undermining our faith in and hope for the promises of God for our future.

PURPOSE REVEALED

One of the greatest weapons against discouragement is a revelation of our real purpose in life. Discouragement wants to blind us to purpose and make life seem meaningless and empty. By contrast, God wants to fill us with vision for our future, because He knows that being convinced of our purpose will give us courage to persevere in life. This is why, throughout the Bible, we see God asking people, "What do you see?" He was asking about their vision, about how they perceived their life purpose. I love what Jeremiah said when God asked him this question:

> *Moreover, the word of the Lord came to me, saying, Jeremiah, what do you see? And I said, I see a branch*

or shoot of an almond tree [the emblem of alertness and activity, blossoming in late winter] (Jeremiah 1:11 AMP).

According to the Amplified Bible, the almond tree symbolizes activity happening in late winter. Prophetically, this meant the breakthrough was coming at what seemed like the end of the season. But God was telling Jeremiah to look with his spiritual eyes and see God's timing for what He was bringing forth. He wants to do the same for us. When we look with the eyes of our spirits, we will be able to discern our true purpose in life. This vision will give us the courage to endure, just like Abraham. Hebrews describes the sacrifices Abraham made because of His forward-looking vision:

> *By faith Abraham, when called to go to a place he would later receive as his inheritance, obeyed and went, even though he did not know where he was going. By faith he made his home in the promised land like a stranger in a foreign country; he lived in tents, as did Isaac and Jacob, who were heirs with him of the same promise. For he was looking forward to the city with foundations, whose architect and builder is God* (Hebrews 11:8-10).

In Abraham's case, he did not even get to see the fulfillment of the vision in his lifetime, but he lived in faith for that vision and was strengthened by it. He lived for a day he would not see but that, through his obedience, he helped to birth. What an incredible legacy! It is no wonder Abraham is called the father of faith. As the apostle Paul wrote, *"Against all hope, Abraham in hope believed and so became the father of many nations, just as it had been said to him, 'So shall your offspring be'"* (Rom. 4:18). Against all reason, in the face of impossibility, Abraham fixed his eyes on the vision God had placed before him, and he refused to become discouraged. As a result, he became the father of Isaac at the age of 100, and through Isaac and his descendants, he became the father of many nations.

Vision is so important. That is why Paul prayed his fellow believers would see the hope of their calling—or God's vision for their lives:

> *I pray that the eyes of your heart may be enlightened in order that you may know the hope to which he has called you, the riches of his glorious inheritance in his holy people* (Ephesians 1:18).

Such vision is the source of great courage and strength. I've experienced this in my own life. After a season of ministry in my twenties, I spent nearly twenty years as a stay-at-home mom to my three children. During the season of motherhood, I had to learn to balance my current season with the calling of God I sensed for a coming season of ministry. It was almost as if I was, inwardly, at two places at once, and at times I felt torn. Part of my destiny was to raise children who will love God and be a light to the world. That was what I was living in during those years. But another part of my destiny involved traveling ministry, teaching, leading prayer meetings, holding conferences, and writing books. I needed wisdom for how to live in the moment and be content, while also living with forward vision for the coming season.

Once, while I was home with the kids, still in my pajamas and cleaning the house, I heard God ask me, "Margie, what do you see?"

In my spirit, I saw myself holding large conferences and ministering throughout the United States. God filled me up with vision for my future that day, and I held that vision in my heart, because it is part of my destiny, even though it was not my experience in that moment. He showed me that my season as a stay-at-home mom would be followed by something else. In that, He gave me the grace to not become discouraged in the present but to engage and treasure it, while also keeping my vision toward the future. This balance between present-moment vision and forward vision reminds me of the incredible ability bald eagles possess of simultaneously seeing forward (binocular vision) and sideways (monocular vision). Bald eagles have great forward-looking depth perception at long distances; they also can see out the sides of their eyes, which gives them the ability to detect motion. What an amazing type of vision that looks both forward and sideways in order to maximize both depth perception and motion detection from great distances.[23]

As humans, our natural eyes do not work like that. We only possess binocular (forward-looking) vision. Yet spiritually, we can and should have both. This will enable us to appreciate both the motion of our current season and the vision of our future season. For most of us, our lives contain multiple seasons in which we walk out our destiny in very different ways. That is why we must run the race of life with patience and discern our current season while also looking ahead with faith for future seasons. It is a delicate balance, at times, but it keeps us from discouragement.

I love the advice God gave the prophet Habakkuk about how to handle vision:

> *Write down the revelation and make it plain on tablets so that a herald may run with it. For the revelation awaits an appointed time; it speaks of the end and will not prove false. Though it linger, wait for it; it will certainly come and will not delay* (Habakkuk 2:2-3).

In these verses, God told Habakkuk to write down the vision clearly and then to wait patiently for its fulfillment at the proper time. Being convinced of God's vision and purpose for our lives is one of the greatest weapons against discouragement. As we keep our eyes fixed on that vision, it is not only sustained, but it grows in our hearts and gives us the courage to wait until we see it manifested.

THE POWER OF HOPE

The difficulty that so many people face when it comes to vision is that, when it seems long in coming, they lose heart and become discouraged. It is as the proverb says, *"Hope deferred makes the heart sick, but a longing fulfilled is a tree of life"* (Prov. 13:12). It is easy to lose hope when our vision for our lives seems to be deferred, or put off to a future time. If we look at our lives from a natural perspective, it can be difficult to see the progression toward our destiny. It is something we must comprehend by faith, based on the promises of God, regardless of what life seems to tell us. That's what Abraham did when, as an elderly and childless man, he hoped for the promised heir.

That is what David did, too, as he waited approximately twenty years between when Samuel anointed him as king and when he actually took the throne of Israel. He spent those years primarily as an outlaw, fleeing for his life from King Saul, yet he found the strength to hope patiently for the fulfillment of all God had promised. Once, while David and his men were at war, some of his enemies raided his home city, Ziklag, and captured all of the women and children. When David and his men returned to find their city burned and their families gone, they wept aloud. The men were so overwhelmed by grief and embittered in their spirits that they talked of stoning David. But in the face of such horrible events, David strengthened himself in the Lord. He found strength in God apart from his circumstances and was able to get direction for how to regain all that had been stolen (see 1 Sam. 30). David knew that giving in to discouragement would only cause greater loss. Instead, he found courage and hope in God, and as a result, he overcame.

In the story of David we see just how effective hope can be as a weapon against the forces of discouragement. The New Testament tells us hope protects our minds and our souls so that we can persevere in our calling. As Paul wrote, *"Let us be sober, putting on faith and love as a breastplate, and the hope of salvation as a helmet"* (1 Thess. 5:8). Hope is a helmet, protecting our thoughts. It is also an anchor for our souls, holding us firm and secure in the middle of life's storms (see Heb. 6:19).

The key to harnessing the power of hope is our faith. In the Old Testament, Solomon wrote that hope deferred disappoints, but in the New Testament Paul wrote, *"Hope does not disappoint, because the love of God has been poured out in our hearts by the Holy Spirit who was given to us"* (Rom. 5:5 NKJV). In Christ, hope does not disappoint. When our eyes are fixed on Him in faith, we can trust that He will lead us into our destiny. We can *"hold unswervingly to the hope we profess, for he who promised is faithful"* (Heb. 10:23). This is the great Christian experience, learning to fix our hope on Jesus, no matter what is happening around us, believing that He is bigger and better than our circumstances. After all, as Paul points out, hope is not hope once it is fulfilled:

> *For in this hope we were saved. But hope that is seen is no hope at all. Who hopes for what they already have? But if we hope for what we do not yet have, we wait for it patiently* (Romans 8:24-25).

Thus, we get to live in the tension of belief in and hope for realities we have not yet seen. As we do, we will get to experience the rich reward of hope fulfilled: *"So do not throw away your confidence; it will be richly rewarded"* (Heb. 10:35).

NEVER GIVE UP

So many believers allow life to discourage them and kill their hope for the future. Certainly, it is not always easy to overcome discouragement. Sometimes our circumstances look very bleak. But the truth is, we also have hope when our eyes are fixed on Jesus. He is the great hope giver and destiny revealer, and when we look to Him, He gives us the courage to soar through the storms of life toward our destiny. Isaiah wrote:

> *But those who hope in the Lord will renew their strength. They will soar on wings like eagles; they will run and not grow weary, they will walk and not be faint* (Isaiah 40:31).

Putting our hope in the Lord enables us to soar like the eagle, who can ascend higher into the sky than most other birds. Eagles also use the pressure of oncoming winds, which are sometimes quite strong, as well as updrafts coming from hills and mountains, to push themselves to higher altitudes. By doing this, they are able to soar across long distances. Using the winds in this way saves a great deal of energy, and the eagles hardly have to flap their wings as they travel.[24] In their example, we can see the truth that every opposing wind that comes against us can be an opportunity for us to rise higher and go farther. Our ability to rise above adversity will determine our ability to succeed. As Rick Joyner has said:

Determine that you will get better, and every mountain you climb will make you stronger. Those who stay resolutely on course to fulfilling their goal, regardless of setbacks and disappointments, are the greatest achievers.[25]

God kept telling Joshua to be strong and have courage, because He knew discouragement would keep them from winning the battle (see Josh. 1:6-18). God's plan for us always involves hope and a good future (see Jer. 29:11); when life looks difficult or seems to threaten our destiny, we need to choose to believe in God's plan and His ability to work it out in our lives. Like the heroes of faith, we need to refuse discouragement and hold tenaciously to hope. When we do, as their example shows us, our hope will not be in vain. As Paul wrote:

> *For everything that was written in the past was written to teach us, so that through the endurance taught in the Scriptures and the encouragement they provide we might have hope* (Romans 15:4).

Our faith in God makes all the difference. For this reason, we should declare over ourselves and others the powerful prayer of Romans 15:13: *"May the God of hope fill you with all joy and peace as you trust in him, so that you may overflow with hope by the power of the Holy Spirit."* Our God is a God of hope, not discouragement, and He promises to fill us with all joy and peace when we choose to trust in Him. His joy and peace will then feed our hope, increasing it to overflowing because of the power of the Holy Spirit at work in our lives. Truly, He can transform our outlook in any situation and empower us with joy, peace, and hope as we look with His vision for the future. If we refuse to become weary, we will reap the promised harvest of destiny in our lives (see Gal. 6:9). We will taste the goodness God has promised us, and it will be worth the wait.

PRAYER OF REFLECTION

I am so glad, Father, that You are the source of all hope and courage. Strengthen me by Your Spirit to refuse to give in to discouragement and to hold resolutely to hope for the future, despite what may be happening around me. Remind me of the reward of faith and perseverance, so that I can keep my vision fixed on You and Your faithfulness in my life.

Chapter 13

---•---

THE TREASURES OF THE WORLD

But the worries of this life, the deceitfulness of
wealth and the desires for other things come
in and choke the word, making it unfruitful.
—JESUS (Mark 4:19)

We live in a world obsessed with material wealth. Many people give the majority of their time to the pursuit of money and the possessions money can buy. Yet, it seems the more people have, the more they want; so, the pursuit of riches never ends. Of course, money itself is not bad. It is a necessary tool for life. But the priority many people place on money is harmful, because it distracts us from the true riches found in the Kingdom of God. When this happens, as Jesus said in Mark 4:19, the deceitfulness of wealth can choke the word of God in our lives, making it unfruitful.

This is true, because whatever we place the highest priority on in our lives becomes our god. If money is our priority—the thing we give the most time and energy to, the thing we dream about and long for—it has replaced God as the one we worship. As Jesus said, *"No one can serve two masters. Either you will hate the one and love the other, or you will be devoted to the one and despise the other. You cannot serve both God and money"* (Matt. 6:24). We can only give our highest worship to one person or thing. That is the nature of worship.

We all face the temptation to prioritize money, because money is an important part of life. We do need it, and God wants to bless us with it. Yet, if our hearts are not fully His, it will make our relationship with Him unfruitful. It will cause us to miss out on our destiny, and the very thing God intended as a tool for the Kingdom will become, instead, an idol in our lives. This is true whether we have a lot of money or not much at all. What makes money an idol in our lives is the posture of our hearts. A wealthy person who is driven to always be accumulating more money may have the same heart posture as a poor person who continually worries about not having enough money. Both have placed their trust in money, and it has become their god.

Whatever we worship will determine our vision for our future. If money is our god, we will focus on it rather than the fullness of God's Kingdom on earth. The question is: Are we God seekers or treasure seekers? Is God or money the source of our hope and security in life? If God has our bank account, He has us. If we have given Him the ability to tell us how to use our money, He knows He has our hearts. The Bible makes it clear He is calling us to a much greater purpose than acquiring possessions. To follow that purpose, we must be free of the love of money.

TREASURE SEEKERS

Jesus faced the same temptations we do, as humans, and this is no exception. During His forty days in the wilderness, the devil took Him to a high mountain and showed Him all the kingdoms of the world and their riches. *"All this I will give you,' he said, 'if you will bow down and worship me'"* (Matt. 4:9). In other words, the devil was offering Jesus all the riches in the world if He would walk away from God's plan for His life. The devil is offering us the same thing today. Perhaps Jesus considered the devil's offer. After all, it would not have been a temptation if the idea was not appealing to Jesus the man. Certainly, possessing power over all the wealth of the world could have been a viable way to influence the world back toward God. And it would have negated the need for the cross.

Essentially, what Satan offered Jesus was the possibility of finding destiny apart from God's plan. Satan was saying, "Jesus, You want to change the world. Here's an easier way to do it. All You need to do is worship me, and I will make it so easy for You." This, of course, was a lie then, just as it is a lie now. We will never reach our destiny apart from God's path, and Jesus knew that. He knew the riches of the world could not purchase the Kingdom of God on earth, and He recognized that it would not really be God's Kingdom if He didn't follow God's path. It would not be God's Kingdom if He chose to worship the devil by placing a priority on money. Thus, Jesus responded with a quote from Deuteronomy 6:13, *"Worship the Lord your God and serve him only"* (Matt. 4:10). Only God is worthy of our worship. The idol of money-chasing may seem to offer us a way to success in life, but it is the same old lie the devil has been telling for years. True success and wealth are found only along God's path for our lives.

The Bible tells us the stories of several individuals who prioritized money above the will of God. Balaam, the seer, was led away by the offer of money, and even though he did not curse the Israelites (because God prevented him), his heart was clearly devoted to the wealth offered him rather than the righteous purposes of God (see Num. 22-24). As a result, he is mentioned several times in the New Testament as an example of the kind of people who are led away from God's will by the enticement of wealth.

Peter talked of those who *"have left the straight way and wandered off to follow the way of Balaam son of Bezer, who loved the wages of wickedness"* (2 Pet. 2:15). And Jude referred to those who *"have rushed for profit into Balaam's error"* (Jude 1:11). In other words, these people value money above God's will. Their focus is on the pursuit of money rather than the pursuit of God's will. As a result, they stray into wickedness and error. Paul put it this way: *"For the love of money is a root of all kinds of evil. Some people, eager for money, have wandered from the faith and pierced themselves with many griefs"* (1 Tim. 6:10). While money is not evil, the love of money is, and it can bring great grief into a believer's life.

We see this, also, in the example of the New Testament church in Laodicea. When Jesus appeared to John and gave him several messages for the early churches of his day, He sent this rebuke to the believers at Laodicea: *"You say, 'I am rich; I have acquired wealth and do not need a thing.' But you do not realize that you are wretched, pitiful, poor, blind and naked"* (Rev. 3:17). They thought their wealth could enable them to control their destiny, to create happiness and security for themselves. But Jesus told them the truth: The poverty of their faith could not be remedied by material wealth. In reality, they were wretched and naked. Their riches could accomplish nothing of value for them if their hearts were not fully devoted to God.

Jesus told a story about a rich farmer who demonstrated the same error. This man had such an abundance of crops that he did not have a place to put it all. So, instead of sharing his wealth with the poor, he decided to build bigger barns, saying to himself, *"You have plenty of grain laid up for many years. Take life easy; eat, drink and be merry"* (Luke 12:19). In response to the man's boasting, God said, *"You fool! This very night your life will be demanded from you. Then who will get what you have prepared for yourself?"* (Luke 12:20). His reliance on himself and his riches was fruitless. Like the angel Lucifer, who thought he could become as powerful as God, the farmer asserted his own will over and over, thinking he had become wealthy enough to determine his own destiny. But in the end, his self-assertions mattered little. In summary, Jesus said, *"Watch out! Be on your guard against all kinds of greed; life does not consist in an abundance of possessions"* (Luke 12:15). And, *"This is how it will be with whoever stores up things for themselves but is not rich toward God"* (Luke 12:21).

Jesus then contrasted this story with the way we should view money in the Kingdom. He pointed to the birds and the flowers and God's provision for them, saying, *"Life is more than food and the body more than clothes"* (Luke 12:23). Because God provides food for the birds and clothes the flowers with splendor, we can trust Him to provide for our needs as well when our hearts are fully His. Jesus continued, *"The pagan world runs after all such things, and your Father knows that you need them. But seek his kingdom, and these things will be given to you as well"* (Luke 12:30-31). In other words, our relationship with the treasures of this world is all about the position of our hearts.

Jesus acknowledged our healthy need for food and clothing and the material things of this world. After all, God created us with physical bodies that have needs for survival and pleasure. This is not bad. The problem is when we do not trust God to provide for our needs and instead take our provision into our own hands. The writer of Hebrews said it this way: *"Keep your lives free from the love of money and be content with what you have, because God has said, 'Never will I leave you; never will I forsake you'"* (Heb. 13:5). It's all about our hearts and where we place our trust.

Jesus wasn't saying we should never work for money or have jobs in order to provide for our families. The Bible makes it clear that hard work and prudence are important (see 2 Thess. 3:10). The issue is, do we trust God's plan for our lives enough to follow His lead, even if it means taking a position that pays less money or refusing overtime in order to spend time with the kids? The most important treasure in this life is our relationship with God and the realities of His Kingdom. When God's will and the coming of His Kingdom on earth are foremost in our hearts and minds, we will be able to relate to money as a tool, not a god. We will prioritize the will of God above the treasures of this world.

SPIRITUAL TREASURE

This is who God wants us to be—people who can handle money righteously, according to His direction. In fact, Jesus said the ability to control money while not being controlled by it actually qualifies us to handle the riches of His Kingdom: *"So if you have not been trustworthy in handling worldly wealth, who will trust you with true riches?"* (Luke 16:11). True riches are the spiritual riches found in relationship with God (see 2 Cor. 4:7; Col. 2:3). Moses, living as the son of the Pharaoh, realized that all the wealth and fame in the world meant nothing if he was not following God's path for his life. As a result, *"He regarded disgrace for the sake of Christ as of greater value than the treasures of Egypt, because he was looking ahead to his reward"*

(Heb. 11:26). He knew the treasures of Christ far surpass those of this world.

This value for spiritual treasure above earthly treasure is the standard for believers. The apostle Paul specifically listed it as a qualification for leaders in the Church:

> *Now the overseer is to be above reproach, faithful to his wife, temperate, self-controlled, respectable, hospitable, able to teach, not given to drunkenness, not violent but gentle, not quarrelsome, **not a lover of money**. He must manage his own family well and see that his children obey him, and he must do so in a manner worthy of full respect* (1 Timothy 3:2-4).

Leaders must measure up to this standard, because they are examples to the Church as a whole. They show us what mature believers in Jesus look like, and the goal is for all of us to live with this godly and healthy perspective toward money. Later in the same letter, Paul addressed the issue of the love of money in more detail, giving this command:

> *Command those who are rich in this present world not to be arrogant nor to put their hope in wealth, which is so uncertain, but to put their hope in God, who richly provides us with everything for our enjoyment. Command them to do good, to be rich in good deeds, and to be generous and willing to share. In this way they will lay up treasure for themselves as a firm foundation for the coming age, so that they may take hold of the life that is truly life* (1 Timothy 6:17-19).

Again, the emphasis is upon trusting in God and His plan and provision rather than in the power of wealth. When we truly trust God, we will have generous hearts and be eager to share what we have. This is how we gain spiritual treasure. One way we enter into more of God and deeper intimacy with Him is through trusting Him more than we trust our bank account and, therefore, living with radical generosity toward others. Then, we will be like the widow Jesus praised. Though she gave only a small amount, it was everything she had. Her trust was in God. Thus, according to Heaven's perspective, she gave more than anyone else: *"They all gave out of their wealth; but she, out of her poverty, put in everything—all she had to live on"* (Mark 12:44).

To those whose hearts were consumed with love for money, Jesus gave this counsel:

> *Sell your possessions and give to the poor. Provide purses for yourselves that will not wear out, a treasure in heaven that will never fail, where no thief comes near and no moth destroys. For where your treasure is, there your heart will be also* (Luke 12:33-34).

In response to the rich young ruler's questions about how to inherit eternal life (true riches), Jesus said: *"One thing you lack.... Go, sell everything you have and give to the poor, and you will have treasure in heaven. Then come, follow me"* (Mark 10:21). The remedy for hearts in love with money is always radical generosity. Letting go of inferior gods makes room for God in our hearts, and we will discover what it feels like to be free from dependence on money. In that place, we will finally be able to seek the Kingdom first. It will become our great treasure, and for it, we will give all we have. As Jesus said, *"The kingdom of heaven is like treasure hidden in a field. When a man found it, he hid it again, and then in his joy went and sold all he had and bought that field"* (Matt. 13:44).

When our hearts are fixed on this greatest of all treasures, we will be positioned to receive and use material prosperity in a way that honors God.

GOD'S PROSPERITY

Some believers, recognizing the dangers of idolizing money, have viewed wealth as an evil. Yet, as mentioned earlier, money is neutral. The issue is always in our hearts. This is important to recognize, because when our hearts are not possessed by the love of money, God actually wants to bless us materially. Not only does He promise to provide for all of our needs (see Phil. 4:19), but He is also the God *"who richly provides us with everything for our enjoyment"* (1 Tim. 6:17). The apostle John prayed for other believers this way: *"Beloved, I pray that you may prosper in all things and be in health, just as your soul prospers"* (3 John 2 NKJV). In other words, as our souls prosper (mature) in love for and faith in God, the "all things" of our lives will also prosper.

What this looks like is different for everyone; the point is, God wants us to prosper. He wants us to have good health and to lack nothing. Paul talked about this when he encouraged the Corinthians to be cheerful givers, saying, *"And God is able to make all grace abound toward you, that you, always having all sufficiency in all things, may have an abundance for every good work"* (2 Cor. 9:8 NKJV). In other words, God wants us to abound in Him—because He loves us *and* because He wants us to use our money as a tool for the Kingdom. When our hearts are right, we will be able to prosper financially without compromising the truth and falling away from our calling. We will be able to use the riches of this world to fulfill our destiny and establish the Kingdom of God on earth.

PRAYER OF REFLECTION

Thank You, Father, for enabling me, as Your child, to worship only You and to trust Your provision in my life. I declare that money is not my god, and my security is not in my bank account but in my relationship with You. Help me to value the treasures of Heaven above the treasures of this world. Teach me to have a right heart toward money and to be radically generous. I want to be someone You can trust to use money for Your Kingdom purposes on earth.

Chapter 14

RELIANCE ON OUR OWN WORKS

There is more in the atonement by
way of merit, than there is in all
human sin by way of demerit.
—CHARLES H. SPURGEON

When God spoke to Jonah the prophet, asking him to preach to the evil city of Nineveh, Jonah ran in the opposite direction. He didn't just refuse to go to Nineveh, but he decided to go to Tarshish instead (see Jonah 1). He ran away from God's presence and tried to make up for it by keeping busy. Many in the Church today are following Jonah's example—running from God's presence and filling their lives with activity instead. People may call this activity "ministry," but that does not negate the fact that it is taking the place of pursuing the presence of God. When we run from His presence, no matter how "good" the things we run toward are, we are choosing to rely on our own might and the strategies of this world instead of the power of His presence. All true ministry is born out of intimacy with God. Without intimacy, our successful projects and checked-off to-do lists don't mean a thing.

DRIVEN BY WORKS

This tendency to focus on doing good works instead of spending time in God's presence is rooted in a belief (conscious or otherwise) that once we are saved by faith we then need to earn God's approval through good works. In a very real way, it is a return to the Law-based system of the old covenant. It is a reliance on our own good works rather than the finished work of the cross. But that is not what Jesus died for. He gave His life to set us free from the Law and empower us to live righteously through relationship with God. Salvation has always been a free gift. The apostle Paul wrote a great deal about this in the New Testament epistles, because he wanted people to understand this truth, which is the foundation of the gospel: *"A person is justified by faith apart from the works of the law"* (Rom. 3:28). We are justified by faith alone.

In his discussion of faith, Paul referred to the concept of *"the righteousness of God,"* which is revealed in the gospel of salvation through faith alone.

> *For in the gospel* **the righteousness of God** *is revealed—a righteousness that is by faith from first to last, just as it is written: "The righteous will live by faith"* (Romans 1:17).

Several chapters later, Paul used this phrase again, saying, *"Apart from the law the righteousness of God has been made known.... This righteousness is given through faith in Jesus Christ to all who believe"* (Rom. 3:21-22). The righteousness of God comes through faith, "from first to last," and it is completely apart from the Law. This idea is so revolutionary, because it contradicts the human assumption that we need to earn God's love and forgiveness. Instead, the truth is: *"God made him who had no sin to be sin for us, so that in him we might become the righteousness of God"* (2 Cor. 5:21). Through faith, not only are we forgiven, but we now embody the glorious truth of the gospel by becoming the righteousness of God. It can be hard for our human minds to comprehend how amazing the gospel really is.

In the next chapter of Romans, Paul continued his discussion of righteousness by highlighting faith as the opposite of reliance on works:

> *To the one who does not work but trusts God who justifies the ungodly, their faith is credited as righteousness. David says the same thing when he speaks of the blessedness of the one to whom God credits righteousness apart from works: "Blessed are those whose transgressions are forgiven, whose sins are covered"* (Romans 4:5-7).

Through our faith in God, our sins are forgiven, and we are made righteous. In the old covenant, people tried to become righteous through obeying the Law, but they could not. Abraham, who predated the Mosaic Law, was considered righteous because of his faith in God (see Rom. 4:3). We in the new covenant have that same blessing of receiving forgiveness and righteousness by faith (see Phil 3:9). What so many Christians miss is that our good works do not make us righteous. Many of the early believers misunderstood this, too, and they began following the Law again, thinking they could earn righteousness through it. However, Paul made it clear that it is not possible to earn righteousness through good works. He wrote, *"If righteousness could be gained through the law, Christ died for nothing!"* and, *"If a law had been given that could impart life, then righteousness would certainly have come by the law"* (Gal. 2:21; 3:21).

Righteousness is only and always a gift from God, based on our faith in Him, which enables us to have intimacy with Him. Then, from that place of intimacy with Him and knowledge of His heart, we partner with Him by doing good works on earth. The first century Church at Ephesus got this backward. To them, Jesus said:

> *I know your deeds, your hard work and your perseverance. I know that you cannot tolerate wicked people, that you have tested those who claim to be apostles but are not, and have found them false. You have persevered and have endured hardships for my name, and have not grown weary. Yet I hold this against you: You have forsaken the love you had at first. Consider how far you have fallen! Repent and do the things you did at first* (Revelation 2:2-5).

They were strong in good works, but they had forsaken their first love. For believers, love must always come first. Good works are important. They're a big part of why we are on earth, but they should never replace our intimate relationship with God. If they do, we are essentially returning to trying to earn our righteousness through works instead of working based on our love relationship with God. It may seem like a slight distinction, but it makes all the difference in our hearts. The question is: What motivates our good works?

DOING GOOD DEEDS

The Bible tells us we are designed to do good works for God's Kingdom. Some people have seen the message of salvation by faith alone as a reason to avoid any works, yet this is a misunderstanding of the gospel message. We are not saved by works, but we are saved by faith, which empowers us to do good works. Paul explained it this way:

> For it is by grace you have been saved, through faith—and this is not from yourselves, it is the gift of God—not by works, so that no one can boast. For we are God's handiwork, created in Christ Jesus to do good works, which God prepared in advance for us to do (Ephesians 2:8-10).

It's not one or the other; it's both, but in the proper order. Relationship with God through faith comes first, but if it is not followed by works, it is not genuine faith. James made this clear when he wrote, *"As the body without the spirit is dead, so faith without deeds is dead"* (James 2:26). Even Jesus did works and pointed to them as proof of His relationship with His Father: *"Do not believe me unless I do the works of my Father"* (John 10:37). In other words, if we say we know God, but we don't manifest the fruit of that relationship through good works, others have reason to question whether we really know God. This is because spending time in His presence fills us with the desires of His heart and inspires us to act according to those desires.

When we love God, it's in our DNA to be workers of righteousness on the earth. Thus, God invites us to partner with Him in establishing His Kingdom through doing good deeds. The New Testament is full of commands regarding good deeds as the outworking of love. Paul told his spiritual son,

Timothy, *"Command them to do good, to be rich in good deeds, and to be generous and willing to share"* (1 Tim. 6:18). Peter added to this the idea that our good deeds can cause unbelievers to glorify God. He told believers, *"Live such good lives among the pagans that, though they accuse you of doing wrong, they may see your good deeds and glorify God"* (1 Pet. 2:12). And James pointed to good deeds as proof of maturity: *"Who is wise and understanding among you? Let them show it by their good life, by deeds done in the humility that comes from wisdom"* (James 3:13).

The need for love-inspired good works is so important that Paul actually said the purpose of the fivefold ministry is *"to equip his people for works of service, so that the body of Christ may be built up"* (Eph. 4:12). Leaders in the Church are called to *"spur one another on toward love and good deeds"* (Heb. 10:24). Of course, the problem comes in when we turn our focus to the works and neglect our relationship with Christ. Our time in His presence must always be most important, because He is the one who fills us with His heart and enables us to work for the Kingdom.

Paul—the great apostle who worked hard spreading the gospel and discipling believers, who wrote a majority of the New Testament books, endured great persecution, and eventually gave his life for the gospel—recognized that all his good works were a result of relationship. About his work as an apostle, he wrote, *"To this end I strenuously contend with all the energy Christ so powerfully works in me"* (Col. 1:29). Paul contended strenuously. He labored for the gospel. Yet, he realized all his hard work was only enabled by the power of God in him through faith in Christ. Thus, he told the Philippians, *"It is God who works in you to will and to act in order to fulfill his good purpose"* (Phil. 2:13). We work because Christ works in us. We work because we love Him, and His love pours out of us in good deeds. We labor because of love, not fear or obligation (see 1 John 4:18). Such love-labor is only possible when we daily spend time in His presence.

KNOWING CHRIST DAILY

The gospel is not about a once-and-done decision; it is about an intimate relationship. If we want to just be good people who do good things, without investing in a personal relationship with God, we are looking back to the Law. Back then, only a few people had a personal relationship with God—people like Moses and Samuel and David. Moses had a reputation as someone who knew God face to face, but the Israelites did not. When Moses entered the tent of meeting to talk with God, the people would stand at their tents to watch (see Exod. 33:8-9). But they never entered into God's presence themselves. In fact, when God offered to make them a nation of priests (give them all relationship with Him), they asked, instead, to have Moses as their mediator (see Exod. 19:6; 20:19). That was the reality under the old covenant, when people attempted to do works of obedience apart from relationship.

But when Jesus came, He invited everyone into intimate relationship with Him. He invited us, like Mary, to sit at His feet and fellowship with Him (see Luke 10:39). When Jesus visited the sisters, Martha and Mary, Martha was working hard in the kitchen, preparing food for her guest, but Mary chose to sit and listen to Jesus. Martha criticized her for this, saying to Jesus, *"Lord, don't you care that my sister has left me to do the work by myself? Tell her to help me!"* (Luke 10:40). The text says she was distracted by the many preparations needed; as a result, her focus shifted from relationship to works. Though Martha had received Jesus into her house, she neglected to actually fellowship with Him. In response to her complaint, Jesus lovingly rebuked her:

> "Martha, Martha," the Lord answered, "you are worried and upset about many things, but few things are needed—or indeed only one. Mary has chosen what is better, and it will not be taken away from her" (Luke 10:41-42).

Mary had made the better choice. When Jesus walked into her house, she sat at His feet. She gave Him her full attention and postured herself for the higher calling—which is intimacy with Jesus. Though I'm sure she also noticed the many preparations needed, she chose to prioritize relationship. In the same way, for us, the lifestyle of intimacy with Jesus, through prayer and fellowship, is always a choice.

Works are important and essential, but daily relationship with God must always have first place in our hearts. The Lord's Prayer speaks of receiving *"daily bread"* from God (see Luke 11:3). At the Last Supper, Jesus referred to the sacrifice of His body on the cross as the bread of our communion with Him (see Matt. 26:26). In other words, the daily bread we receive from Him is our relationship with Him. Daily, we need to come into His presence and meet with Him. That relationship is the prize He died to give us.

When we meet with Him daily, we are choosing to depend on our relationship with Him, not on our works. Only faith in Him saves us and makes us righteous. Only the grace we find when we rest in His love empowers us to do the works of our Father. That is why Jesus invited us into the lifestyle of secret prayer, where no one but God sees what we're doing. Jesus told the works-driven Jews of His day:

> Be careful not to practice your righteousness in front of others to be seen by them.... When you pray, go

into your room, close the door and pray to your Father, who is unseen. Then your Father, who sees what is done in secret, will reward you (Matthew 6:1,6).

This is still true for us today. When we meet with God in the place of secret prayer, we demonstrate the priorities of our hearts. There, we commune with Him and learn to know Him as our Father and our friend. This is the sort of relationship Jesus talked about when He told His disciples, *"I no longer call you servants.... Instead, I have called you friends"* (John 15:15). Yes, we are still God's servants, who do good deeds for His Kingdom. But foremost, we are friends; we are those who receive His love and learn to love Him back, and out of that place of communion with Him, we are inspired to do good works. All true ministry is born from our love for God and love for His people.

PRAYER OF REFLECTION

Father, thank You for giving me salvation and righteousness based on faith alone, not on works! Help me to remember that I never need to work to earn Your love or approval. Instead, help me to make my relationship with You my first priority. I want to daily spend time in Your presence. I want the good works I do to be inspired by Your love for me and my love for You. Help me to make this a daily reality in my life.

Chapter 15

———————•———————

WEARINESS

There is no good time to learn about resting. There will always be something that will prevent you from resting. Psalm 46 opens with an earthquake and ends with, "Be still, and know that I am God."
—GRAHAM COOKE

Weariness is a temptation we all face at times, especially when God's promises seem to be long in coming, the Kingdom work we're doing feels difficult or unrewarding, or we face opposition. As a traveling minister, I am friends with many pastors and their spouses. I love fivefold pastors dearly. They have a parental heart of love, they are patient and discerning, and they truly care about their people. In my traveling ministry, I don't have to deal with the daily activities involved in working with the same people over an extended time. They, on the other hand, see the same people every week, know about the ups and downs of their lives, and truly care about them. In my experience, many of them, at times, become discouraged, tired, and weary because they don't always see the numerical growth they hope for in their churches.

Because of this, God often uses me to speak words of encouragement into their lives and to remind them to focus on the vision He has given them. Vision is so important. When pastors drift away from their vision, that's when they are most prone to discouragement. I also remind them that, in God's eyes, true spiritual authority has nothing to do with how many people fill up a church on a Sunday morning. Some of the largest churches in America exercise little or no spiritual authority in the realm of the spirit in comparison to some smaller churches who are exercising their faith and praying with spiritual authority. Over and over, I have seen that returning, in faith, to look at the vision causes strength to arise and discouragement to leave. This is not only true for pastors and leaders but for all believers.

The Bible tells us we do not need to give in to weariness, even when it's knocking at our door. In Christ we have the patience and strength we need to endure and keep pressing forward, with our eyes fixed on the vision God has placed before us. Paul promised the early believers, *"But the Lord is faithful, and he will strengthen you and protect you from the evil one"* (2 Thess. 3:3). The same is true for us today. By His grace, we can be unflinching in our resolve.

Habakkuk, the Old Testament prophet, knew what this patient endurance was like. God spoke to him about the future and told him:

> *Write down the revelation and make it plain on tablets so that a herald may run with it. For the*

*revelation awaits an appointed time; it speaks of
the end and will not prove false. Though it linger,
wait for it; it will certainly come and will not delay*
(Habakkuk 2:2-3).

When it felt as though the promise was lingering and
might never come, God told Habakkuk to wait for it with
faith, because it would certainly come. We need this same
sort of endurance in our own lives if we want to pursue our
destiny. God's plans for our lives are fulfilled over a lifetime,
which means sometimes it feels like they're taking a long
time. Sometimes we doubt whether they will happen at all. At
those moments, we need to choose whether we will agree with
discouragement and weariness or with God's promises.

Though weariness is the road of less resistance, because
it does not require us to stand strong in faith, it is also the
more dangerous, because it distracts us from God's vision
for our lives. It blurs our focus and turns our eyes away
from Jesus. Instead, we find ourselves focusing on our circumstances—how hard life is and how tired we feel. While
life may be hard and we may feel tired, those realities do
not diminish God's vision for our lives. He is the author and
finisher of our faith, and He wants to strengthen our hearts
to persevere. As Paul the apostle promised, *"When you are
tempted, he will also provide a way out so that you can endure it"*
(1 Cor. 10:13).

Jesus never promised living life or fulfilling destiny
would be easy. Actually, He said, *"In this world you will have
trouble. But take heart! I have overcome the world"* (John 16:33).
We can take heart because of His promises and because
of the victory of the cross. We do not need to be overcome
by weariness, but we can overcome weariness by the grace
of God.

LIVING FROM REST

This is why, when Jesus called people to follow Him, He told them about His ability to free us from weariness: *"Come to me, all you who are weary and burdened, and I will give you rest"* (Matt. 11:28). The antidote to weariness is the emotional and spiritual rest we find in Christ. This rest isn't necessarily about what we are or are not doing but about the position of our hearts. When our hope and faith are fully fixed on Jesus and His promises, we will not strive in our work, and we will not become weary.

Simply put, rest is a position of trust. When we fully trust God, we are at rest in His goodness. The author of Hebrews wrote an entire chapter about rest, showing how we are able to enter into God's rest in the new covenant: *"There remains, then, a Sabbath-rest for the people of God; for anyone who enters God's rest also rests from their works, just as God did from his"* (Heb. 4:9-10). This rest is synonymous to relying on God's strength instead of our own. It means resting in Him and His promises in faith rather than overworking and striving in an attempt to fulfill our destiny on our own. This makes rest a powerful spiritual weapon, because it is agreement with God's will in God's way.

The apostle John said we can know our hearts are at rest in God's presence when we genuinely love others, not just with our words but with our actions.

> *Dear children, let us not love with words or speech but with actions and in truth. This is how we know that we belong to the truth and how we set our hearts at rest in his presence* (1 John 3:18-19).

The connection here is simple. Rest involves letting go of agendas and trusting in God. When we do that, loving others the way He loves us is simple, because we are content to follow His lead and love the one in front of us, regardless of how it may or may not seem to fit with our destiny.

THE PRACTICE OF REST

Of course, sometimes we manifest our spiritual position of rest in God by practicing physical rest. Many Christians do not understand the importance of physical rest. They see the spiritual as being more important than the physical, and as a result they do not take good care of their bodies. The long-term effect of this is not just poor health but a deteriorated ability to persevere and prosper in our souls. However, if God did not care about our physical bodies and needs, He would not have created us with the three-part nature we have. He does not only care about our spiritual health, but also about our emotional, mental, and physical health. Rest plays a big part in all three of these areas of our lives. We cannot thrive emotionally, mentally, or physically without the proper amount of rest in the form of sleep and relaxation.

In my own ministry, God spoke strongly to me about my need to take more time for physical rest and fun. This may seem unspiritual, but it is not. For example, I find that when I am physically tired or haven't slept properly, my lack of rest opens a door for thoughts of discouragement. These discouraging thoughts are not based on reality but simply on my need for a good night's sleep or a restful vacation! But if I'm not aware of that, they can easily distract me from what God has put before me. When I am tired, I also have more difficulty discerning the enemy's lies and resisting the distractions and warfare he sends my way. Truly, we cannot overestimate the importance of sleep to our holistic welfare.

Some other religions in the world value asceticism and self-denial, but the Bible gives us a much more balanced view on life. In it, we find Jesus and the leaders of the early Church making provision and giving instructions for spiritual growth in a holistic manner, involving our emotional, mental, and physical needs. For example, right after the twelve apostles returned from a ministry trip, Jesus took them away to a solitary place so they could eat and rest:

> *The apostles gathered around Jesus and reported to him all they had done and taught. Then, because so many people were coming and going that they did not even have a chance to eat, he said to them, "Come with me by yourselves to a quiet place and get some rest." So they went away by themselves in a boat to a solitary place* (Mark 6:30-32).

Jesus knew that our ability to minister and thrive spiritually is closely connected to rest. What is truly unhealthy is attending to only one part of our selves while neglecting the others. Rest keeps us balanced. Even in the most intense situations, rest matters. Soldiers in human armies do not fight constantly. They have seasons of battle and seasons of rest. The same applies to all areas of life. We are not made to run full-force ahead for long periods of time. Instead, we need to recognize that, in order to give God our best, we actually must rest. That rest is also a part of our spiritual warfare and mission, just as eating is part of an athlete's performance. When a marathon runner is sitting and eating, it may not seem like he is actively in the race, but he is, because his preparation for the actual running—through good eating—is what will enable him to persevere and win.

In the same way, as Christians who are running the race of life, we need to live balanced lifestyles that consistently make a place for rest—not just sleep but also fun and relaxation. By doing this, we are sowing into our ability to persevere for God and fulfill our destiny in Him.

MOVING FORWARD

When we live from a place of spiritual rest in Jesus and also take time to physically rest, we will be well-equipped to persevere in the midst of life's difficulties. We will have the spiritual, emotional, mental, and physical stamina to keep moving forward in obedience to God's call. This is so important, because a lack of perseverance can cause us to lose out on what God wants to give us and accomplish through us. Paul made this clear when he wrote: *"Let us not become weary in doing good, for at the proper time we will reap a harvest if we do not give up"* (Gal. 6:9). If we do not give up, if we do not give in to weariness, we will reap a harvest.

This reality does not mean we should feel shame if we have given in to weariness in the past. God can redeem any situation, and He loves to take our failures and turn them around for blessing. However, sometimes we do miss out on specific blessings that God wanted to give us, if only we had persevered. Scripture makes it clear—enduring to the end is crucial: *"If we endure, we will also reign with him. If we disown him, he will also disown us"* (2 Tim. 2:12). This reality should encourage us to persevere like Jesus did, even in the midst of great difficulty:

> *Let us run with perseverance the race marked out for us, fixing our eyes on Jesus, the pioneer and perfecter of faith. For the joy set before him he endured the cross, scorning its shame, and sat down at the right hand of the throne of God. Consider him who endured such opposition from sinners, **so that***

you will not grow weary and lose heart (Hebrews 12:1-3).

Keeping our eyes on the example of Christ and resting in His ability in us will rescue us from weariness and the temptation to lose heart and give up on the vision He has placed before us. This is not always easy. Sometimes, it is very hard, especially if we have not regularly practiced holistic rest in our lives. Yet Jesus, the source of all rest and hope and faith, promises to renew and strengthen us inwardly, every day, so we can keep our eyes fixed on what is unseen and eternal:

> *Therefore we do not lose heart. Though outwardly we are wasting away, yet inwardly we are being renewed day by day. For our light and momentary troubles are achieving for us an eternal glory that far outweighs them all. So we fix our eyes not on what is seen, but on what is unseen, since what is seen is temporary, but what is unseen is eternal* (2 Corinthians 4:16-18).

He has already provided the strength we need. He has already put His Spirit and truth within us so that we may be *"strengthened with all power according to his glorious might so that* [we] *may have great endurance and patience"* (Col. 1:11). The key to perseverance is resting in God's goodness and promises, even when they are part of the unseen realm and have not yet manifested in our lives. Even the great apostle Paul did not know all his life had accomplished or how he would attain all God had called him to. Probably, none of us ever do in this life. Instead, we are given a choice: We can walk in faith, persevering and pressing on toward our high calling, or we can give up because of weariness and doubt.

Runners are trained to run with their focus on a point beyond the finish line so that they will not slow down as they reach the finish line but continue on. The same principle applies to us. None of us knows exactly what our end will look like or when we'll cross the finish line of our personal lives, but we can fix our gaze on the eternal Kingdom purposes of God on earth. We can focus on the call to become like Him and do the works He did. When we run toward these goals, which are beyond the span of our individual lives, we will not fall short or slow down at the end. Instead, we will run whole-heartedly, with perseverance, until we leave this earth.

Too many great Christians have stumbled or lost their zeal toward the end of their lives, because their gaze was not fixed on a mark beyond the finish line. We must not repeat their mistakes but must train ourselves to run toward a vision that surpasses our individual lives—to run consumed by the vision of Jesus glorified and the Kingdom of God on earth as it is in Heaven. When we fix our eyes on Heaven's goals, while resting in the goodness of God, weariness will not be able to keep us from our destiny.

PRAYER OF REFLECTION

Father, thank You for providing the grace I need to persevere in any situation. Help me to live a lifestyle of rest and faith in You, so that I do not become overwhelmed by setbacks or difficulties or delays. You are the author and finisher of my destiny, and I know I can rest in Your promises to complete the good work You have started in me. Please show me, also, how to incorporate physical rest into my life so that I am able to endure to the end.

CONCLUSION

Many Christians have the mistaken notion that
eternal life begins when they die. But that is
not biblically accurate. Eternal life begins when
we are born again into the Kingdom of God.
—DAVID JEREMIAH

We can live our lives with one of two focuses—our temporal
life on earth or the eternal life we receive when Jesus enters
our hearts. We can live for the seen or the unseen realm. It's
up to us. But the choice we make will make all the difference
in our relationship with God and our ability to fulfill His plan
for our lives. He loves us just as we are, no matter what we do,
but He wants us to engage His heart for His Kingdom on this
earth. He invites us to be part of His glorious eternal plan.

Whenever I attend a funeral, I am reminded of what matters most in this life. I am reminded that life is about so much
more than the days and hours we spend on this planet. My
purpose here is bigger and more glorious than I know, and
it's because Jesus has invited me to be an ambassador and

co-laborer for His Kingdom. This reality recalibrates my focus. I know one day I too will make the transition from this life to the next. Thus, focusing on the things of this world will profit me nothing in the end. When I go to Heaven, I cannot take anything from this world with me. But I can leave a legacy in this world of the goodness and power of God. I can leave lasting fruit for His Kingdom that will continue to bear fruit and multiply long after I'm gone. That is my goal.

If that's your goal, too, I'd like to invite you to spend the next thirty days praying through each of the prayers at the end of the chapters in this book. Be sure to also write down anything you may see with the eyes of your spirit as you pray. I believe these short prayers will help recalibrate any areas of distraction in your heart and refocus your vision toward eternity.

ENDNOTES

1. *Strong's Exhaustive Concordance,* s.v. "Zoe," #G2222.

2. "Peregrine falcon," *Department of Environment and Heritage Protection* (Queensland Government, 2014); https://www.ehp .qld.gov.au/wildlife/livingwith/peregrine_falcon.html (accessed Dec. 16, 2014).

3. Alan Rabinowitz, quoted in Maryann Mott, "Did Animals Sense Tsunami Was Coming?" *National Geographic News* (Jan. 4, 2005); http://news.nationalgeographic.com/news/2005 /01/0104_050104_tsunami_animals.html (accessed Dec. 18, 2014).

4. Kenneth E. Hagin, *I Believe in Visions* (Broken Arrow, OK: Faith Library Publications, 1972), 47-48.

5. Winifred Gallagher, *Rapt: Attention and the Focused Life,* reprint (New York: Penguin, 2010), Introduction.

6. The word translated as "trance" in this verse is the Greek word *ekstasis. Strong's Exhaustive Concordance,* #G1611.

7. "Cheetah," *National Geographic;* http://animals .nationalgeographic.com/animals/mammals/cheetah/ (accessed Dec. 17, 2014).

8. Stefan Swanepoel, "Serengeti Skill #3: The Efficient Cheetah," *Surviving Your Serengeti: 7 Skills to Mast Business and Life;* http:// www.serengetibook.com/your-safari/what-animal-am-i /cheetah/ (accessed Dec. 17, 2014).

9. Jessica Kleiman, "How Multitasking Hurts Your Brain (and Your Effectiveness at Work)," *Forbes.com* (Jan. 15, 2013); http:// www.forbes.com/sites/work-in-progress/2013/01/15/how -multitasking-hurts-your-brain-and-your-effectiveness-at -work/ (accessed Dec. 17, 2014).

10. Timothy Ferriss, quoted in Eric Barker, "6 Things the Most Productive People Do Every Day," *Barking Up the Wrong Tree* (June 1, 2014); http://www.bakadesuyo.com/2014/06/most -productive-people/ (accessed Dec. 17, 2014).

11. Eric Barker, "Stay Focused: 5 Ways to Increase Your Attention Span," *Barking Up the Wrong Tree* (Sept. 18, 2013); http://www .bakadesuyo.com/2013/09/stay-focused/ (accessed Dec. 17, 2014). Each of the five points comes from Barker, but the reflections on these points are mine.

12. Peter Gambaccini, "After Bleak Year, Ryan Hall has 'Grown in Perseverance,'" *Runner's World* (Dec. 17, 2013); http://www .runnersworld.com/elite-runners/after-bleak-year-ryan -hall-has-grown-in-perseverance (accessed Dec. 19, 2014). You can follow the journey of Ryan and his wife, Sara (also a professional runner), on their website, http:// ryanandsarahall.com.

13. Mike Bickle, "The Free Gift of Our Greatness," *The Elijah List* (Dec. 12, 2003); http://www.elijahlist.com/words/display _word/1814 (accessed Dec. 22, 2014).

14. Rick Warren, *The Purpose Driven Life* (Grand Rapids, MI: Zondervan, 2002), "Day 19: Cultivating Community."

15. *Strong's Exhaustive Concordance*, #H2731.

16. Ibid., #H4170.

17. Jamie Buckingham, *Daughter of Destiny: Kathryn Kuhlman* (Alachua, FL: Bridge-Logos, 1999).

18. Kenneth E. Hagin, *Growing Up Spiritually* (Broken Arrow, OK: Faith Library Publications, 1976).

19. Jeffrey Kluger, "The Happiness of Pursuit," *Time Magazine* (July 8, 2013); http://content.time.com/time/magazine/ article/0,9171,2146449,00.html (accessed Oct. 28, 2014).

20. Joseph Mattera, "Why God Doesn't Care If You're Happy," *Charisma News* (Sept. 9, 2014); http://www.charismanews.com /opinion/45319-why-god-doesn-t-care-if-you-re-happy (accessed Oct. 29, 2014).

21. Hagin, *I Believe in Visions*, 86.

22. Joyce Meyer, *Battlefield of the Mind* (New York: Warner Faith, 2002).

23. "Frequently Asked Questions about the Bald Eagle," *Hancock Wildlife Foundation* (2010); http://www.hancockwildlife.org /forum/viewtopic.php?showtopic=949 (accessed Oct. 31, 2014).

24. "Bald Eagle Facts: Q & A with Peter Nye, New York Department of Environmental Conservation," *Learner.org* (2006); http://www.learner.org/jnorth/tm/eagle /ExpertAnswer07.html (accessed Oct. 31, 2014).

25. Rick Joyner, *The Call* (Fort Mill, SC: MorningStar Publications, 2006).

ABOUT MARGIE FLEURANT

Author, speaker, and founder and president of The River Ministries, Margie Fleurant speaks in the prophetic voice, challenging and building up the Body of Christ through keen biblical insights. Margie's messages and books inspire and ignite a deeper passion for pursuing the presence of God. In them people discover how to study and meditate on Scripture in order to uncover a more vibrant faith and intimate prayer time with the Lord. All of her teachings are grounded on the timeless principles of the Word of God. She often teaches on how to hear and understand the heart of the Father and how to realize His desire to see His people fulfill their ordained purposes here on earth.

Prayer is the cornerstone of The River Ministries, and Margie has shared the importance of prayer with congregations throughout the United States and overseas. Margie is a woman who is uncompromisingly devoted to preaching the Gospel message with authority and simplicity. The revelations she shares bring power and victory to people of faith no matter how long they have been on their spiritual journey. Traveling extensively as a keynote speaker, Margie uses the prophetic gifts God has given her to creatively share messages with youth and adults in relevant ways. She has been the main speaker at many churches, women's conferences, leadership conferences, and youth conferences throughout the United States.

Margie graduated from Rhema Bible Training College in 1977 and is an ordained minister through Covenant Ministries International, Sayreville, New Jersey. She is also an ordained member of Faith Covenant Ministries. Margie and her husband, John, currently reside in New Jersey and have three grown children.

OTHER TITLES BY MARGIE FLEURANT

DECISION TIME

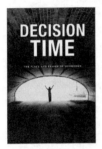 When we say yes to His call to surrender, He will stir up the hunger in our hearts for more of Him. We will learn to know Him more deeply and intimately in that brand-new place of saying yes to His grand plan. In that new place of wholeness and intimacy, He will be able to lead us into the fullness of destiny. We will discover our part in His plan and begin to walk it out faithfully. He desires to use us to accomplish great things, if only we will say yes to His call. His plan for our lives may not be easy, but it will be great, because through it we will be enacting His eternal plan.

A LOVE LIKE THAT

 *A Love Like That* is Margie Fleurant's latest hardcover book release. This hardcover edition will increase your understanding of how much the Lord loves each one of His precious daughters.

Each one of us has a story. Our lives are like history books—with accounts of victory as well as pain, happy times and tearful times. No matter what our history has been or where we are in the progression of our story, when we encounter the love of God we are changed. The old chapter ends, and a new chapter begins. God does not hold on to the past, but He promises to do a new thing in us. That is what this book is all about.

As you encounter God's love through the pages of this book, you will experience freshness, newness, wisdom, and increased revelation. You will discover how to be consumed with God's love, how to be changed by His perfect love, and how to continue to grow in His love throughout your life.

Discover how you can have a deeper, tender spiritual relationship with God and learn practical ways to grow closer to Him.

MARKED FOR INTERCESSION

Discover the doorway into the mightiest release of power known to man. This power is released through the art of intercession. God is searching for men and women who will walk in their authority and fulfill the great commission in the secret place of prayer. You will learn how to pray the appropriate prayer for the need at hand and how the Holy Spirit can be vitally involved. This type of prayer will effect change on the behalf of individual lives, your home, churches, cities, and nations.

This is the second edition of *Marked for Intercession*.

PRAYER FOR THE MINISTRY GIFTS

A book written specifically for ministry leaders. Church leaders need the appropriate prayer support from faithful congregants. In this book, gain insight into how the call of God affects the heart of a minister. Discover how this call motivates the leader as you prayerfully support them in fulfilling their destiny, affecting the church body as a whole.

ENCOUNTER GOD THROUGH THE HABIT OF PRAYER

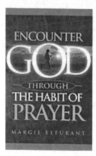

Many people possess a certain reverence for God, yet they view Him as a distant personality who's disinterested in the daily activities of their lives. Many are going through life unfulfilled, their spiritual hunger unsatisfied. They haven't learned the truth that God desires to walk with them in real, intimate fellowship. Learn how to experience a matchless companionship with the Lord that is anchored in prayer and vital to the human experience.

THE ART OF INTERCESSION STUDY GUIDE

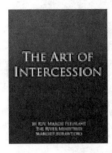

This is a detailed study guide for people who want to dive in to God's Word and study the topic of prayer. In this booklet, readers will learn about the different kinds of prayer, the foundations needed for prayer, and the power being an intercessor allows you to tap into as you pray to the Lord.

To purchase additional teaching materials or to schedule a speaking engagement, please contact Margie at:

www.MargieFleurant.org